CALLED IN CHRIST

Our privileges and opportunities as God's children

Robert Folkenberg

Pacific Press Publishing Association
Boise, Idaho
Oshawa, Ontario, Canada

Edited by David Jarnes
Designed by Dennis Ferree
Cover art by Darrel Tank
Typeset in 11/12 Janson Text

Unless otherwise indicated, all Scripture references are from the New International Version of the Bible.

Library of Congress Cataloging-in-Publication Data:
Folkenberg, Robert, 1941-
    Called in Christ : our privileges and opportunities as God's
children / Robert Folkenberg.
        p.   cm.
    ISBN 0-8163-1203-6
    1. Identification (Religion) 2. Christian life—1960-   I.
Title.
BV4509.5.F585   1993
248.4—dc20   93-21392
                                                        CIP

93 94 95 96 97 ● 5 4 3 2 1

Contents

Preface

God calls *us*—what a wonderful thought! He calls us to be His own, to walk with Him, to serve Him, to represent Him, to grow into His likeness. As once Jesus walked by the Sea of Galilee and challenged Peter, James, and John, "Follow me," (Matthew 4:19), so we hear His voice in our time. Will we, like those fishermen of old, rise and follow Him, forsaking all?

God's call doesn't just come in general terms. He calls us to live a very special life. The Scriptures make clear the precious truth that He calls us to live our lives "in Christ." We have just two options. According to the Bible, two individuals—Adam and Christ—sum up and comprehend all those who have ever lived on earth. "For as in Adam all die, so in Christ all will be made alive" (1 Corinthians 15:22). We are all *in Adam* by reason of our birth—in him in sin and death. But the glorious truth of the gospel is that Jesus died for us all—and we were *in Him* on the cross! God has made righteousness and life available to us—to those who are in Him.

The chapters that follow describe various experiences to which God calls us—or various aspects of His call. As you read these chapters, I would urge you to keep one vital point in mind: every call is *in Christ*. Only in Christ can we repent, find assurance, be victorious and compassionate, witness, await His coming, be revived, and triumph. Only in Christ—never in ourselves.

Two explanatory notes regarding material used in this book: First, I want to give credit where credit is due. Some doctrinal sections of the chapters that follow depend quite heavily, if indirectly, on the General Conference Ministerial Association's book *Seventh-day Adventists Believe . . . A Biblical Exposition of 27 Fundamental Doctrines.*

And second, some readers may not be acquainted with Ellen G. White, from whose works I have drawn one chapter of this book and whom I quote frequently in the chapters I wrote. Ellen White (1827-1915) was one of the early founders of the Seventh-day Adventist church. Seventh-day Adventists believe she experienced a modern manifestation of the prophetic gift. Although we don't consider her writings to be on a par with the Bible, we have greatly benefitted from the wise spiritual counsel she gave.

As I prepared these chapters, I spent much time in prayer. Dear friend, will you join me in earnest prayer as you read them? Will you pray for yourself, that you may follow God's call to you? Will you pray for those who have been called to leadership, that we may serve in the spirit of the Master? Will you pray for God's church, that we all may press together in love, unity, and heart-searching for a closer walk with Him?

As long as we choose Christ, we remain in Him. And He is mighty to save and mighty to keep! May this book draw us all closer to heaven and closer to one another.

Robert S. Folkenberg, President
General Conference of Seventh-day Adventists

1

Called to Repentance— in Christ

Biblical repentance never goes out of style.

"*Repent!*" cries the preacher on the street corner to passing students and shoppers. "*Repent or be damned!*"

But the crowds barely notice him; the words he speaks through his battery-operated public-address system do little more than add to the din of the city. His message falls on the stony ears of people who prefer more palatable ideas—like "Live up to your human potential!" "Don't let anybody make you feel guilty," and "There are no sins, only lifestyle choices."

Repentance is definitely out of fashion.

But when Noah stood on the steps of the ark and preached to the scoffers, his message was not "Something good is going to happen to you!" King Jeroboam didn't order Amos out of town because the prophet was proclaiming "God's in His heaven, and all's right with the world." Jeremiah wasn't thrown into the pit for preaching "I'm OK, you're OK." Nor was the sermon that got John the Baptist beheaded based on the theme "Smile, God loves you!"

No, the messages of all these men of God can be summed up

in one word: "Repent!" They didn't think repentance was out of style. They talked about it a lot. Nor is the call to repentance just an Old Testament message. It's true that the New Testament introduces the era of grace. But grace without repentance is, as Dietrich Bonhoeffer says, "cheap grace." Grace without repentance is no grace at all. It is, instead, simply a whitewash. The message of the New Testament—the message of the gospel—is, in fact, also a message of repentance.

The New Testament preachers consistently preached it:

■ Both John the Baptist and Jesus consistently warned, "Repent, for the kingdom of heaven is near" (Matthew 3:2; 4:17).

■ The disciples "went out and preached that people should repent" (Mark 6:12).

■ At Pentecost—and on other occasions—Peter proclaimed, "Repent and be baptized, every one of you, in the name of Jesus Christ for the forgiveness of your sins" (Acts 2:38; see also Acts 8:22; 2 Peter 3:9).

■ Paul reported, "First to those in Damascus, then to those in Jerusalem and in all Judea, and to the Gentiles also, I preached that they should repent and turn to God and prove their repentance by their deeds" (Acts 26:20).

■ And John the Revelator recorded the message Jesus sent through him, "Those whom I love I rebuke and discipline. So be earnest, and repent" (Revelation 3:19).

Indeed, from Genesis to Revelation, God's message to man is *Repent!*

Repentance Is Good News!

So when the street preacher proclaims "Repent or be damned!" he has the message right. But the preacher's technique could use some refining. He makes the call to repentance sound like a threat—as though God is vengeful. However, "God did not send his Son into the world to condemn the world, but to save the world through him" (John 3:17). Jesus said, "The time has come

. . . The kingdom of God is near. Repent and believe the *good news!*" (Mark 1:15, emphasis supplied). Repentance is part of the gospel, the "good news." Good news!

In what way is the call to repentance good news? It's good news because it helps us make sense of what we see on the newscasts and read in the papers. It's good news because it helps us understand what's going on in our own lives. It's good news because it says God sees possibilities for good in what otherwise appears to be a hopeless situation.

All history seems to be the record of battles—nations and ethnic groups fighting for land, resources, or just plain power. On the personal level, we've gotten so used to an increasing crime rate that we're satisfied if it doesn't grow any faster than inflation. And the violence that pits nation against nation and race against race seems to have struck at families as well. Too often now, husband is pitted against wife and parents against their own children.

What's the source of all this anger, this hatred, this evil? The Bible says the evil disease now ravaging our world first appeared long ago, in the very heart of our universe. Lucifer, one of the beings God created and commissioned with a high position in His government, became proud. Consumed by ambition, this angel who later came to be known as Satan attempted to displace God, to himself become god (see Ezekiel 28:12-17; Isaiah 14:12-14).

Not content to carry on his struggle against God alone, Satan began to seek support among the other created beings of his rank. Revelation indicates that he won a third of the angels to his side (see chapter 12:4, cf. 1:20). Losing what had become an open war against God, he and his angels turned their attention to this world. They would seek support among people, beings created in God's image. Genesis 3 tells the familiar story of Eve and Adam, the serpent and the forbidden fruit. Satan tempted them to distrust God and to grab divine prerogatives for themselves. The heads of our race succumbed. And the Bible makes the consequences clear: Life became a struggle. But more significantly, self-centeredness became the prime motivator. And violence soon followed—when, in anger, Cain killed Abel.

Anyone who's had to say "I'm sorry" to husband or wife,

parents or children, friends or neighbors, knows we've been scarred by the battle Lucifer began in heaven. Every war, every violent crime, every blow struck, every angry word, every hateful thought reveals the power of Satan's influence in this world. Created in God's image and intended to live our lives in relationship with God, we ignore Him—if we don't live in outright rebellion against Him. Made to love as He loves, we cheat and slander and lie and steal and kill. Meant to live eternally, we struggle through a few years and then die.

As technologically advanced as our civilization is, we've found no antidote for what's wrong with ourselves. Our social sciences and man-made religions can salve some of the symptoms and sometimes slow the progress of the disease. But they haven't found the cure for the ailment. Without outside intervention, we're doomed.

That's why God's call to repentance is good news. It says that He's able to do something about our condition—and just as importantly, that He considers us worth the effort.

A Precious Gift of Jesus

Admitting our problem is the first step to discovering God's solution. All the power of heaven becomes available to those who choose God's side in this great conflict of the ages. But by nature we're deeply mired in sin. Where, then, does the desire to repent come from? It's as much a precious gift of Jesus as is the pardon that follows it.

Marjorie Camper illustrates this truth with an experience she shared with her six-year-old son. One spring day the two of them were out in their garden. While Mrs. Camper was absorbed in her gardening, the little boy explored the plants practically exploding into life everywhere around him. He picked a daffodil bud and sat down on the ground to study it. Impatient to see the full flower, he tried to force it into full bloom with his two little hands—only to see it fall to pieces. Frustrated, he cried out, "Mommy, look! How does God open it into a pretty flower?" Then, before his mother could answer, he drew his own conclusion: "Oh, I know! God works from the inside."

Repentance is a seed that grows in the soil of a heart that is warmed by the presence of Jesus, a heart that is stirred by the realization that He provides the only solution to our problems. It isn't a mask to cover our sins. It is a desire for change, a willingness to abandon those sins through Jesus' power.

And all of us have felt His call. Jesus said, "But I, when I am lifted up from the earth, will draw all men to myself" (John 12:32). We may resist this love; we may refuse to be drawn to Christ—but all those who don't resist *will* be drawn to Him. As Paul declared, God's kindness leads us to repentance (see Romans 2:4). The drawing power of the Holy Spirit is one of His greatest gifts. As we respond, we become more sensitive to His presence.

But though repentance is a gift God wants to give all people, we may not receive it. Why? Thomas Carlyle said, "Of all acts of man, repentance is the most divine. The greatest of all faults is to be conscious of none." Therein lies the problem. For the most part we ignore calls to repentance because of common pride. Few of us admit, even to ourselves, that we need to change. "Rich and increased with goods and in need of nothing" (Revelation 3:17, KJV) describes too many within and outside the church.

Have you ever argued with a friend over some issue, certain that you were right—only to discover later that you were wrong? I've had that experience. I've lost my patience with my children, spoken harsh words to a colleague, said something unkind to my wife, and then had to say, "I'm sorry. I was wrong; you were right." That's very hard to do. The degree of difficulty we feel in repenting is a measure of our pride.

We find it far more comfortable to blame a parent, blame heredity, blame the system, blame a junk-food diet—blame anyone or anything but ourselves for our shortcomings. You see, pride rejects repentance as unnecessary and demeaning to self-esteem. It doesn't recognize that repentance is Christ's prescription for peace.

A Repentance That Doesn't Ring True

Sometimes, however, we do repent—but with a repentance that doesn't ring true. Expediency may pull from us a reluctant or false repentance that is really no repentance at all. Such was the repentance forced from Pharaoh's proud heart when the plagues fell on Egypt. "Then Pharaoh summoned Moses and Aaron. 'This time I have sinned,' he said to them. 'The Lord is in the right, and I and my people are in the wrong' " (Exodus 9:27). Judas experienced a similar "repentance" when he realized what he had done in leading the mob to Christ. " 'I have sinned,' " he said, 'for I have betrayed innocent blood' " (Matthew 27:4). And the Old Testament character Achan's repentance, voiced when his breaking of God's explicit command had been uncovered, reeks of the same stench. "Achan replied, 'It is true! I have sinned against the Lord, the God of Israel' " (Joshua 7:20).

On Achan's confession, Ellen G. White offers these insights:

> There is a vast difference between admitting facts after they have been proved and confessing sins known only to ourselves and to God. Achan would not have confessed had he not hoped by so doing to avert the consequences of his crime. . . . His confession only served to show that his punishment was just. *There was no genuine repentance for sin, no contrition, no change of purpose, no abhorrence of evil* (*Patriarchs and Prophets*, p. 497, emphasis supplied).

Like Achan, Pharaoh and Judas admitted they had sinned. But they were no more repentant than he. They had no change of heart. They regretted only that they had been caught—like people who get speeding tickets, pay the fines, and then buy radar detectors to make sure they don't get caught again.

Sometimes parents inadvertently teach that kind of repentance by forcing their children to say "I'm sorry" when they've done something wrong. When the children have had a fight, they command, "O.K., now tell your brother [or sister] you're sorry!" How different is the "I'm sorry" growled through clenched teeth from the sincere "I'm sorry" said with tears in the eyes and voice, the confession that arises from a heartfelt conviction of sin. True repentance arises from a realization of and deep regret for the pain our words or actions have caused others. If the sorrow we feel arises merely from our fear of the consequences to us rather than concern for the consequences to our Lord, it's obvious we'll have no motivation to change. But, as Ambrose of Milan said, "True repentance is to cease from sin."

To bring forgiveness, confession must be specific as well as genuine. It must be more than just a general, blanket confession—you know, the kind that you make when you pray, "Dear Father, if I made any mistakes today, forgive me." Such ritual prayers reveal that we're not really sorry for our sins—that we don't know, or worse yet, don't care, what they cost heaven.

When our prayers become formalities rather than the cry of our broken hearts, eventually we are tempted to stop praying. Such formality was common in Martin Luther's time, when many people regarded sin as a matter of entries on a balance sheet God kept in heaven—entries that a person could change by the purchase of certificates of "indulgence" that the church sold. Luther fought against this idea. He said that sin wasn't just a matter of accounts, it was a matter of relationships—our relationship with God. And the ninety-five theses he nailed to the Wittenberg church door reveal how important he thought repentance to be. His first thesis read: "When our Lord and Master Jesus Christ said 'Repent,' He willed that the entire life of believers be one of repentance."

Jesus also was concerned about meaningless prayers. He said, "And in praying do not heap up empty phrases as the Gentiles do; for they think that they will be heard for their many words" (Matthew 6:7, RSV).

Through God's Eyes

In our world, repentance doesn't come easily or naturally. The problem is that our society not only condones sin, but glorifies it. Our culture has grown so accustomed to the dark that it doesn't even realize the lights are out.

Television and motion pictures present a parade of people who have lost the power of astonishment at their own actions; people who have lost their sense of propriety—who, rather than repenting of their sins, flaunt them under the label "alternative lifestyles." We are living in a new Dark Age. And since there is no sense of the sinfulness of sin, there is no inclination to repent.

"But," said Christ, "I, when I am lifted up from the earth, will draw all men to myself" (John 12:32). Our fundamental problem is that we see the world through our own eyes rather than through God's eyes. When our perspective on life's values is drawn more by merchants of vice than by Jesus, when our view of life is shaped more by the secular world than heaven's values, when everything is lifted up except Jesus, then the heavenly becomes common and the eternal loses its appeal.

We will realize the sinfulness of sin only when we spend time with Jesus, really getting to know Him, becoming acquainted with the depths of His love for us and His sorrow when we remove ourselves from Him. Then our reaction to our failings will be "How can I break the heart of One who loves me so?" We won't regard anything that breaks our relationship with Jesus as "only a little sin." More than anything else, we will delight to live in harmony with Him.

One of the classic biblical stories of repentance is the story Jesus told of the Pharisee and the tax collector (see Luke 18). Jesus aimed this parable at those who were confident of their own righteousness and looked down on everybody else. "Two men," He said, "went up to the temple to pray, one a Pharisee and the other a tax collector. The Pharisee stood up and prayed thus with himself, 'God, I thank You that I am not like other men—extortioners, unjust, adulterers, or even as this tax collector. I fast twice a week; I give tithes of all that I possess.' And the tax collector, standing afar off, would not so much as raise his eyes to heaven, but beat his breast, saying, 'God be merciful to me a sinner!' I tell you, this man went down to his house justified rather than the other; for everyone who exalts himself will be abased, and he who humbles himself will be exalted" (Luke 18:10-14, NKJV).

The part of the story I like best is the line: he "went home justified." It tells me there *are* answers to the problems we face. There *is* such a thing as forgiveness, a new start, a new life.

The poor, deluded Pharisee wanted to remind God of all his good points and to assure himself that all was well. He went home with his sins covered with only a thin veneer of man-made righteousness. Such a veneer eventually cracks. All who attempt a life of self-dependence, seeking to live apart from God, and recognizing no need for repentance, remove themselves from the source of life.

The tax collector went home too, but with his problems solved. His heart must have been as light as a feather. He "went home justified."

Would you rather take home what the Pharisee had or what the tax collector received? Would you like to experience God's justification? Take a moment just now to tell Jesus how you would like to have the same experience with Him that the tax collector had. Tell Him all your troubles. He sees your circumstances and knows all your temptations and sorrows. Then you can tell the one who tempts you to doubt God's forgiving grace that you know your garments are stained with sin, but that by faith you claim the righteousness of Christ.

Let's go home with light hearts—joyful because the Lord is merciful and has forgiven us. Then we can, as the next chapter points out, live in full assurance of salvation.

2

Called to Assurance— in Christ

How to be certain of salvation.

I took off from Guatemala City at 2:00 a.m. in the mission's plane, a Piper Aztec, headed for Sacramento, California. The shortest route to the first stop, Acapulco, Mexico, led directly across six hundred miles of ocean. On approaching Tapachula, the coastal town that was to be my last land checkpoint for several hours, I could see that it was covered by a towering thunderstorm. Bypassing it to the west, I struck out across the Gulf of Tehuantepec.

But my attempt to fly around the storm proved futile. Just beyond this first storm was a second one, and behind that one a solid line of storms. The menacing fifty thousand-foot clouds off my right wing spewed lightning. (I found out later that the storms were the tail of a hurricane that I had not been told about during my preflight weather briefing.) The line of storms blocking my flight path stretched west as far as I could see. Eventually, I was going to have to fly through them because I certainly didn't have enough fuel to go around them if that meant, as it might, flying all the way to Hawaii!

17

When my radio indicated I was over the Pacific directly west of Acapulco, I chose an area in the clouds that had not flashed for a while and flew into the blackness. The needle in my vertical-rate-of-speed indicator jumped wildly between the top and bottom pegs as updrafts and downdrafts exceeding six thousand feet per minute (more than sixty miles/one hundred kilometers per hour) threw my plane about. Then a stroke of lightning burst in such brilliance that I was momentarily blinded. For a few minutes I had to depend on the sound of the engines to control the aircraft. What a relief when about fifteen minutes later I flew into the clear on the other side of the storm!

Feeling physically insecure is bad enough, but feeling spiritually insecure is worse. David learned that after his adultery with Bathsheba. So did Saul as he searched out the witch of Endor. Sometimes a specific sin lies behind our spiritual insecurity, but more often it comes because of a vague anxiety about whether we are going to make it to God's kingdom.

Have you ever heard the phrase "blanket insurance policy"? Such a policy covers everything—like a blanket. Rather than a blanket *insurance* policy, we need a blanket *assurance* policy. We need to sense that in Christ, we have complete assurance coverage.

We've seen that repentance is the sincere and heartfelt response of those who, under the influence of the Holy Spirit, recognize their sinful condition and yet by faith accept God's unconditional love and forgiveness. Such repentance, coming from hearts filled with the love of Jesus, will open the door of our lives to spiritual assurance.

Those who don't experience the assurance of salvation suffer anxiety and guilt. Jesus doesn't want us to live with those emotions. He wants us to feel secure in His love. So He offers us a blanket assurance policy. "My sheep," He says, "listen to my voice; I know them, and they follow me. I give them eternal life, and they shall never perish; no one can snatch them out of my hand" (John 10:27, 28).

Notice what Jesus says: "No one can snatch them out of my hand." That's heavenly security! Some people have shied away from this text because there are those who use it to teach "once saved, always saved"—that once people are saved, it is impossible for them to be lost. Their concern about that idea is justifiable. People certainly can choose to remove themselves from their secure position in Christ. But though some might misuse this text, that's no reason for us to miss out on the blessed assurance it offers. Think of it! Jesus is assuring us that no power on earth or in heaven can remove us from security in Him as long as we choose Him. We may choose to leave Him, but no one can force us to leave Him. As long as we choose to stay in Him, we are secure.

Persevering Faith

The righteousness that qualifies us for heaven is Christ's righteousness, and that Satan cannot touch. But the faith that makes that righteousness effective is in us, not in heaven. It is that faith in God that Satan attempts to destroy. As long as our faith perseveres, our assurance in Christ is guaranteed. That is why Jesus said only those whose faith endures unto the end will be saved (see Matthew 10:22).

When my son Bobby was just a child, he and I visited the tiny San Blas island of Pidertupo in the country of Panama. On a pitch-black, starless night, as we stepped out of a thatched house to walk the narrow trail to the little hut where we were staying, Bobby whispered to me, "Daddy, I'm scared. I can't see." Then he reached for my hand, and when his hand was tucked securely in mine, I heard him say softly to himself, "There, now I can see." Bobby lost his fear when he felt secure.

It is not God's will that we walk on an insecure tightrope balancing our way to heaven, unsure of whether He will open the door when we arrive. Does God invite us to "approach the throne of grace with confidence" (Hebrews 4:16) and then leave us to worry about whether He accepts us? Does Jesus say, "Whoever comes to me I will never drive away" (John 6:37), and then, when we come, leave us troubled about whether we will be turned away? Did God inspire John to say, "I write these things to you who believe in the name of the Son of God so that you may know that you have eternal life" (1 John 5:13), only to pull that security out from under us?

Some might say, "We know God is faithful. We're not insecure because of something Jesus said, but rather because of what we do! It's our sin that makes us insecure. We know that salvation was ours when we received Christ—but we've sinned since then. Where does that leave us?"

We fall into this kind of insecurity when we understand the gospel as conditional good news, as if salvation were like a game of tag: those who've been tagged by sin and haven't had a chance to clear it when the game ends, lose. Or like a game of musical chairs—those who wish to win must be close to a chair when the music stops, to have their last sins confessed before they die. Such approaches to salvation leave us feeling as though we're walking a tightrope of insecurity, never sure of our standing with God.

If our salvation depends only on avoiding certain behaviors, then we will find security only as we perfectly avoid those behaviors. And the list of forbidden behaviors can grow extremely long. But if sin is more than just behavior, if it is losing faith in God, then we can find security by getting into a right relationship with Him. That relationship will provide the spiritual direction we need. And it will provide assurance in Christ because it's not the occasional good deeds or misdeeds we do that reveal our character and our relationship to Christ, but the overall balance of our words and acts and the direction they reveal our lives to have taken.

The gospel is simple. We come to Jesus, confess our sins to Him, and ask Him for both faith to believe His promise that He accepts us and power to live for Him every day. He covers us with His righteousness and assures us that He will complete the work of grace He has begun in us. When we violate His standards, we can turn right to Him; He'll forgive us and give us peace.

One day a man driving along a road in his truck noticed some boys with heavy backpacks hiking the direction he was headed. Deciding he'd help them, he pulled the truck onto the shoulder and asked if they'd like a ride. They said that would be great, showing their appreciation with huge smiles. When they had climbed into the back of the truck, the driver started off. But glancing into his rear-view mirror a few miles down the road, he noticed that the boys were still wearing their packs. Stopping the truck again, he suggested that they take the heavy loads off and make themselves more comfortable. To this suggestion, one boy responded, "No. We really appreciate the ride. The least we can do is carry our own packs."

How foolish—thinking they were doing the truck driver a favor by carrying their own backpacks! But when it comes to eternal life, our own reasoning is often just as foolish. Jesus gives us eternal life as a gift, but we still insist on carrying our own packs. We get into the truck—the church—but we continue to carry our burdens of guilt, sin, and fear of the judgment. The good news is that Jesus gives us eternal life—today. We actually uplift Christ and His righteousness when we lay down our burdens and trust Him and His promises in our everyday life. The peace and restfulness we experience endorses to others what trusting Him does for us.

"Cheap Grace" versus Insecurity

Throughout history people have taken different—and opposing—approaches to assurance. Some have feared that talking of the security of salvation and assurance in Christ leads to "cheap grace" and an inappropriate tolerance of ongoing sinful behavior. So when speaking of salvation, they stress the importance of our obedience.

Others fear that talking of obedience and victorious Christian living directs people's attention away from Christ's gift, focusing it on our lives—which, no matter how saintly we are, fail to meet His standards. They fear the resulting insecurity, the lack of assurance and peace of mind. So they emphasize God's part in salvation.

The concerns of those who hold each viewpoint are understandable—but there's no need to go to either extreme. It would be an aberration of truth for God's children, while claiming assurance in Christ, to persist in sin knowingly or, even more dangerously, to rationalize their way into a lifestyle contradictory to God's expectations. Assurance in Christ must never become an excuse for either licentiousness or spiritual lethargy. The way we live reveals how genuine is the faith we profess.

But the idea that no one can snatch the saved from Jesus' hand should be of great comfort to each of us. Ellen G. White wrote of the peace that it brings:

> The sinner who comes to Christ in faith is joined soul to soul with his Redeemer, united in holy bonds with Jesus. . . . Through faith and experience he has confidence that Jesus not only will but *does* save him to the uttermost. *This confidence brings to his soul an abiding trust, a peace, a joy, that passeth understanding.* (*Signs of the Times*, August 3, 1891, emphasis supplied.)

God wants us to know where we stand with Him. Like Bobby in the dark of the night, we all need to feel secure.

In some ways, our salvation experience is like a marriage. Certainly, no marriage relationship is perfect. True as that is, if you should ask someone whether he or she is married, that person is not likely to respond "I hope so" or "I'm working on it" or "I try to be." In a sense, we are married to Christ, so when we're asked if we are secure in that relationship, we don't have to say "I think so" or "I am working on it." Insecurity denigrates God's gift of righteousness.

Were we given salvation because of our good deeds? Was the prodigal son welcomed home because of his good deeds? No! Salvation is based on grace, not on good deeds. We were reconciled to God by the death of His Son while we were, as Paul wrote, "powerless," "ungodly," "sinners," His "enemies" (Romans 5:6-10). We come to God "just as we are."

Now, if we don't receive salvation because of our good deeds, can we lose it through doing bad deeds? Yes—and no. We obtain salvation through agreeing to enter a relationship of trust in Jesus, and occasional good deeds or misdeeds neither make nor break that relationship. The plain truth is that we only lose salvation when we lose faith in our Saviour. As Paul says, "Everything that does not come from faith is sin" (Romans 14:23). But when we abandon that relationship, sinful acts inevitably follow. So persistent sinful acts are symptoms of a broken faith relationship with Jesus.

Does God condone sinful conduct? No. He's provided the forces of heaven to give us victory over sin. But we must never fall into the trap of considering that victory over sin the source of our salvation. Jesus, through His life and death, has made salvation available to us as a gift. When our relationship with Him is the most important matter in our lives, then salvation is ours. And then, as corollaries, through the power of the indwelling Spirit that we receive, obedience and the overcoming of sin that yields a Christlike life, result.

Please understand, I am not suggesting that behavior is unimportant. The itching sore spots the disease of measles produces on our skin are something to be concerned about. They tell us that something is wrong and that it's time to go to our physician. We're right to want to be rid of them. But we'd be making a mistake if we treated them without treating the disease that causes them.

Our misdeeds are like those measles spots. They irritate us, and we're right in desiring to be rid of them. But they're not the whole problem. They're symptoms, telling us that something is wrong for which we need to go to Jesus to find healing. When we go to Jesus with hearts broken in repentance, He forgives us—healing the inner sickness—and provides us power to overcome.

So finding peace and assurance is not primarily a matter of producing, through grit and determination, good deeds and eliminating wrong deeds from our lives. It's primarily a matter of entering and maintaining a relationship with Jesus.

Entering God's Rest

The New Testament book of Hebrews tells us a lot about assurance. Throughout the book, we're encouraged to learn from God's Old Testament people and their experiences. Chapters 3 and 4 focus particularly on the time when Moses led the Israelites, newly freed from slavery in Egypt, to the borders of the land where God had promised to make them a nation.

Hebrews reminds us God vowed that generation of Israelites would never enter His rest—in other words, the land He had promised them. The problem? Unbelief had led to rebellion and disobedience. The Israelites had been slaves to the Egyptians for years. Then, through a series of miracles, God freed them from their captors and provided their food and drink in the middle of a desert. And by means of cloud and fire, He led them to the border of the rich land where He meant to plant and tend them, growing them into a great nation.

At the border, God had Moses send a representative from each of the tribes through the land to report on the prospects. They came back saying it was all that God had promised. But ten of the twelve "spies" added that the people who lived there were strong and the cities well fortified—the Israelites would never be able to take the land from them.

At this news, the Israelites fell to unbelief. They forgot all that God had done for them up to this point—that the only way they'd gotten where they were now was through His help. Rebellious, they refused to go any farther, saying that instead they intended to return to the land of their slavery, Egypt. Then, when they heard what the consequences of their rebellion would be—forty years in the desolate wilderness—they rebelled again. Missing the point again that it was *with God's help* that they could have taken the promised land, they attempted to win it through their own efforts, even though God told them that was futile. Needless to say, their invasion failed. The people they tried to conquer threw them back across the border.

When the full forty-year sentence had been served and the nation had been renewed by the death of the unfaithful generation, Joshua led the new generation of Israelites to the border of the promised land. Their faith held, and God brought them in. The crossing of the Jordan River and the taking of Jericho show that God's work underlay their success. And the debacle at Ai reminded them—as it reminds us—that human effort alone will not suffice.

Hebrews, however, says that though the Israelites finally entered the promised land, God has an even better country in mind for them—and us (see chapter 4:8; cf. 11:10, 13-16). But those who want to enter that "rest," that heavenly country, the city Abraham sought by faith, must learn to "rest" in Him now.

What does that mean?

As we've seen, it means trusting God. The Israelites Moses led distrusted God in two ways. First, they thought what He offered impossible of attainment. They distrusted His intention and His aid. Second, when they turned from that form of disbelief, they jumped right into another. This time they trusted *themselves* rather than *God* to get what He had promised them.

Hebrews further explains this idea of resting in God by linking it to the Sabbath and Creation. The very word *Sabbath* means "rest." Hebrews says, "Anyone who enters God's rest also rests from his own work, just as God did from his" (chapter 4:10). Humans didn't get into the original Paradise through their own efforts. They neither created nor earned it. That beautiful garden was God's gift to them. He did the work and created them just in time to share His finished Creation. Then He invited them to enjoy with Him the rest that marked the completion of His work. Similarly, God's offer of eternal life in the restored Paradise comes as a gracious gift. We can neither create it nor earn it by our efforts. It's available only as we rest in Him, trusting His creative, saving work for us.

The seventh-day Sabbath (Saturday) is a rest day memorializing both the creative and saving aspects of God's work for us. Exodus 20:8-11 tells us: "Remember the Sabbath day, to keep it holy. Six days you shall labor and do all your work, but the seventh day is the Sabbath of the Lord your God. In it you shall do no work. . . . For in six days the Lord made the heavens and the earth . . . and rested the seventh day. Therefore the Lord blessed the Sabbath day and hallowed it" (NKJV, see also Deuteronomy 5:12-14). So observing it is not legalism. It's not a means of working our way to heaven. In fact, God intends Sabbath-keeping to be just the opposite of that. It's a weekly reminder that to attain salvation, we must rest in God.

But, resting in God, trusting Him, doesn't mean doing nothing. It means that, unlike Israel at the Jordan, we follow His lead—even when what He asks seems impossible. Rebellious disobedience, refusal to follow, reveals that there's a problem with our relationship with God. We're not trusting Him.

Judgment-Day Confidence

Scripture tells us we must all stand before God's judgment seat. Paul told the Corinthians: "We must all appear before the judgment seat of Christ, that each one may receive the things done in the body, according to what he has done, whether good or bad" (2 Corinthians 5:10, NKJV, see also Romans 14:10). That thought scares a lot of people. But the book that assures us God works for the salvation of those who trust Him also offers assurance about the day of judgment. Much of the book of Hebrews was written to tell us that Jesus functions as our heavenly advocate. In effect, that means that during the judgment He will be the lawyer for the defense—*our* defense, if we're resting in Him.

And we have every reason to turn our cases over to Him. He's perfectly qualified to represent us. Hebrews points out that, as the Son of God, He's far superior to any human or even angel we could ask to take our case. Yet, this "high-powered attorney" knows how to represent us well, because He became a human being Himself. That's reason to "approach the throne of grace with confidence, so that we may receive mercy and find grace to help us in our time of need" (Hebrews 4:16).

The apostle John links our relationship with Jesus directly to confidence in the day of judgment. He says that God has given us eternal life—it's in His Son. Whoever has the Son—whoever is resting in Him—has life (see 1 John 5:11-13). Like Hebrews, John points out that realizing this gives us confidence in approaching God (see verse 14). And more to the point, he says it also gives us "confidence on the day of judgment" (chapter 4:17).

There's a modern parable about a man who had twin sons who were the pride of his life. Thinking of all eventualities, he prepared a will and in it established a trust fund so the twins would have money when they needed it—should something happen to him—as they started their own families. Then, soon after the twins' twentieth birthday, the man was killed in an accident.

The trust fund this man had established contained a provision which specified that when the boys turned twenty-one, they were each to be given a new car. They were to go to the local Mercedes-Benz dealer and pick out a car of their choice. On that special birthday, Tom, one of the twins, went to the lawyer who administered the trust agreement and asked if it was true that he could get a car of his choice at the Mercedes-Benz dealership. The lawyer assured him it was true.

But Tom wasn't sure about all this. It sounded too good to be true. So he went to the local bar association to obtain references on the lawyer who was handling the trust account. He learned that his lawyer was a member—in good and regular standing—of the bar.

Still not satisfied, he went next to the public library to study wills and trusts. He found many cases in which relatives had contested trusts and had them nullified. This information worried Tom, and he began to study into the matter even more deeply—spending weeks that stretched into months on the problems children had with parents' wills. He soon became an authority on contested wills and trusts.

As Tom's worries about whether he would ever get his own Mercedes-Benz increased, he called the lawyer again and asked him a series of questions: Was the will properly witnessed? Was it notarized? Had his father signed all the pages? Were any pages missing?

Receiving satisfactory answers to all these questions, he asked if any relatives had contested the will or sought to delay its execution. "None," the lawyer replied. Were the resources in the trust fund adequate to cover the cost of a new Mercedes-Benz? "Easily," the lawyer responded.

When Tom hung up the phone, he considered going to the dealership and picking out a car. But then he thought there must be more to getting a new Mercedes than this, something was bound to come up. Several more months went by as he pondered his next step.

One evening, he walked out of his house in turmoil. It had been a year since he turned twenty-one, and he still didn't have a new car. As he walked along the street, he saw his brother, Bill, whom he hadn't seen since their father's funeral. Bill was driving a beautiful Mercedes-Benz.

"Where'd you get that?" Tom asked.

"Why, the trust fund! Didn't you know? Didn't the lawyer tell you?"

"Yes," Tom replied, "but I was never too sure about it. A lot of wills are contested in court, you know."

"Tom!" Bill said. "In the will, Dad instructed the lawyer that the offer for the new car was good for only one year. It's too late now. The year is over!"

"I knew that it wouldn't work out," Tom replied. "I just knew something would go wrong."

The promise is there, my friends. Won't you take advantage of God's promise now? Don't wait another moment. We uplift Christ and His righteousness by claiming Him, His promises, and the assurance He provides for each of us. When we do so, we will "rejoice in the Lord always" (Philippians 4:4, KJV).

The Christian walk begins with repentance, and repentance leads to assurance in Christ. With that assurance comes a life of victory. We will learn more about that in the next chapter.

3

Called to Victory— in Christ

Complete in Him.

John struggles with lustful thoughts. He knows Jesus said such thoughts are as bad as the act of adultery itself, and he's prayed frequently that God would deliver him—but he still struggles. It seems that God hasn't answered his prayer for victory. What should he do?

Cheryl doesn't get along with her mother. She always determines that the next time her mother comes for a visit will be different. But every time they're together for more than an hour, they get into an argument, and Cheryl ends up saying things she regrets—things that don't, as the commandment says, honor her mother. Like John, she's prayed about this problem regularly. But that hasn't seemed to help.

Fred's concerns aren't as specific as John's and Cheryl's. He doesn't have a "sin" that controls his life. He attends church regularly and donates time, energy, and money to it. But he's still uncomfortable about his spiritual state. While he believes he lives a relatively good life, he knows he still makes mistakes. He wishes the life he's living were more consistent with Bible principles.

Should Christians feel the way John, Cheryl, and Fred do? After all, Jesus offers forgiveness. We've experienced that. And we know the futility of legalism, of trying to meet God's requirements on our own. Haven't the Ten Commandments been done away with for people who accept Christ's death for their sins? Just what does the Bible say about God's law? And what does that law have to do with our lives today?

Confusion About God's Law

Paul, the apostle whose books are most often used to suggest that God's law no longer applies to Christians, wrote that God "forgave us all our sins, having canceled the written code . . . that was against us and that stood opposed to us; he took it away, nailing it to the cross" (Colossians 2:13, 14). But he also wrote, "Do we, then, nullify the law by this faith? Not at all! Rather, we uphold the law" (Romans 3:31).

Contradictory? No.

But confusing? It can be.

To understand what Paul and other biblical writers have to say about the law, we must first understand what they mean by the term *law* itself. Sometimes they're referring to what most people probably think of when they hear the word *law*: the Ten Commandments. But at other times, they mean everything contained in the five books of Moses (Genesis, Exodus, Leviticus, Numbers and Deuteronomy). And on still other occasions they mean by the term the idea that people can merit or buy salvation by law-keeping.

The Ten Commandments differ significantly from the other laws given in the Old Testament. The Ten Commandments are broad, guiding principles that specify how people are to apply God's rule of love to their relationships with God and with other people. The other laws are much more detailed and, for the most part, specific to the nation of Israel. They lay out the rules for the Israelites' religious practices and civil life and provide guidance in matters of sanitation and health.

The Bible carefully distinguishes between the Ten Commandments and these other laws. It says God Himself spoke the commandments to His people and then wrote them on stone—

an indication of the permanence He intended them to have. In contrast, the other laws recorded in the Old Testament were given through Moses, and he wrote them on perishable materials. The Ten Commandments were placed inside the sacred chest in the house of worship. The other laws were stored outside that chest (see Deuteronomy 31:25, 26).

But the nation of Israel played a different role in God's plan than do nations today. So while we can learn from the civil laws that governed it, governing a contemporary nation by those laws would be a mistake. The New Testament also makes clear that the Christian religion supersedes that practiced by the Israelites. We can learn about God by studying the "ceremonial" laws that governed the ancient Israelite religion, but those practices were a "shadow" of the realities that came in Jesus' life, death, and heavenly ministry for us now. So we needn't follow those ceremonial laws. (See, for instance, Colossians 2:14-17; Hebrews 10:1.)

Jesus had quite a bit to say about the law of God. But nowhere did He suggest that Christians need no longer heed it. In fact, in His Sermon on the Mount—which lays out the principles of His kingdom—He said we are accountable to the law for our thoughts and motives as well as our deeds (see Matthew 5:17-30). And He confirmed the law's role as the criterion for salvation (see Matthew 19:16-18).

If you want to know what a nation is like, you can get a pretty good idea by looking at that nation's laws—at least, those laws the nation actually practices. Similarly, God's law reflects His character. It lays out the two basic subdivisions of the principle of love upon which He founded His kingdom. Those two parts are: love God supremely, and love your neighbor as yourself (see Luke 10:27).

The Bible describes God's law as perfect, pure, holy, just, good, true, eternal, and righteous. This law defines a person's duties toward God and other people. Breaking it, according to the New Testament, constitutes sin (see 1 John 3:4).

But doesn't Romans 10:4 say Jesus is the *end* of the law? Yes. But it goes on to say He is the end of the law *for righteousness* to all who believe in Him (KJV). It doesn't say that God has thrown the law out or that He no longer considers it important. It says Jesus has made it clear that people find approval in God's eyes *because of their faith in Him* rather than through attempts to keep the law perfectly—attempts that, since sin entered this world, have always proved futile.

After you walk from your car to a photography studio on a windy day, you check your hair in a mirror to see if it's messed up before you allow the photographer to take your picture. If, however, you find that the wind has ruffled your hair, you don't use the mirror to remedy the situation. You use your comb or brush.

The apostle James says the law is like a mirror (see James 3:25). It shows us when things in our life are not as they should be. That's the role of the law. It tells us something's wrong. But it can't fix the problem for us. That's the role of the gospel, of Jesus. Those who accept Him as Lord and Saviour are no longer under the law, but are under grace. That is, they're no longer under the law's condemnation. Grace provides forgiveness for our breaking of the law, it breaks sin's dominion over us, and it gives us the strength to overcome sin's power (see Romans 8:1; 6:4, 13, 14).

So, can those who have committed their lives to Jesus ignore the law? No. Grace isn't a license to sin. Those who love God will want to please Him (see 1 John 5:3; John 14:15), and He still values the law. It still pictures the ideal kingdom of love He wants to establish, the ideal lifestyle for those who believe His way is best. And just as obeying the physical laws of the universe blesses us with continuing physical life and health, so obeying these spiritual laws continues to be the means to blessings like peace, wisdom, Christlikeness, longevity, and happiness.

Weak People

But what about John, Cheryl, and Fred? They've accepted Christ, they've experienced His forgiveness, and they want to please God. But they're finding themselves weak, unable to live in harmony with the law—even though they agree it's good. How can we obtain victory over our sins? How can we live in harmony with God's good law?

To one extent or another, we've all experienced the feelings these three have. And when we look to the Bible for answers, sometimes we can find statements that perplex us further. It sets a pretty high standard for us: "Be perfect, therefore, as your heavenly Father is perfect" (Matthew 5:48). When we look honestly at ourselves, we realize that we're far from reaching that standard. We find that Paul's analysis fits our situation more accurately: "We know that the law is spiritual; but I am unspiritual, sold as a slave to sin. I do not understand what I do. For what I want to do I do not do, but what I hate I do" (Romans 7:14, 15).

We know what we ought to be doing, but we seem powerless to do it—whether it's eliminating troubling behavior or adding good behavior. Victory escapes us. The discouraging cycle of attempts and failures finally leads us to conclude that we continually experience defeat for one of two reasons. Either we're not sincere enough when we ask for victory—it's our fault! Or God doesn't want to give us the victory—it's God's fault!

We know we really shouldn't blame God, however, so we draw the only other possible conclusion: We're not sincere enough when we ask for victory. It's our fault. This thought only deepens our discouragement. Now, besides struggling with the original problem, we've been made conscious of our lack of faith as well.

So how can we find victory, "sanctification," a new life that releases us from the power of sin and guilt and frees us to love God and serve our neighbors?

Christians have argued long and loud about the answer to this question. I believe that the first step not only to answering the question but also to experiencing the victory comes in defining two words: "sin" and "righteousness."

What is sin? The Bible relates sin to breaking the law: "Whosoever committeth sin transgresseth also the law: for sin is the transgression of the law" (1 John 3:4, KJV). So we tend to conclude that sin is simply the acts God has forbidden in His law—theft, murder, adultery, covetousness, lying, and so forth. Then to "be perfect" as our "heavenly Father is perfect" (Matthew 5:48), we must stop committing these sinful acts. Generally, our attempts to reach that objective involve something along the lines of making a checklist of our sins and then crossing them off as we quit doing them. The more things we quit doing, the more nearly perfect we are. When we've finally stopped committing all sinful acts—presto, we're perfect—or as some say, sanctified!

This approach of defining *goodness* as the avoiding of *badness* causes a number of problems.

First, it suggests that the more sins we conquer, the more nearly perfect we are, and then that the more nearly perfect we are, the less grace we need. Eventually, this line of reasoning goes, we'll be perfect and we won't need any more grace—and then we'll be ready to be taken straight to heaven.

Second, those who hold this view but aren't successful at conquering sin, like Jim, Cheryl, and Fred, get lost in hopelessness and despair. On the other hand, those who hold this view and *are* successful at eliminating sins from their life—or who think they are—tend to become modern versions of the Pharisee in Jesus' story about the Pharisee and the publican. Like many of the other Pharisees of His day, this Pharisee developed inflated views of his own goodness and tried to build himself up by pointing out how bad others were. Neither of these approaches results in confident Christians who rejoice in victorious living.

But "sins" aren't really the problem. They're only symptoms of the problem. "Sin"—with a capital S—is the problem. Becoming Christlike, living in harmony with God's law, isn't simply a matter of stopping sinning. Yes, that's right—I said the solution is not simply to stop committing sinful acts. Rather, it's to dig out the root of *Sin*.

You see, the real sin problem resides in our nature. The apostle Paul realized and admitted that: "But I see another law in my members, warring against the law of my mind, and bringing me into captivity to the law of sin which is in my members" (Romans 7:23, KJV). It was his realization of how deeply rooted sin is in our lives that led him to cry out, "O wretched man that I am! who shall deliver me from the body of this death?" (verse 24, KJV). Clearly, he saw the problem as far more serious than merely the sinful acts we do.

The Old Testament prophets also recognized the fact that sin is rooted in the deepest core of our being—our hearts. Jeremiah said, "The heart is deceitful above all things, and desperately wicked: who can know it?" (Jeremiah 17:9, KJV). Every one of us who looks deep into our own hearts will see evil thoughts and motives. I don't simply mean evil deeds that we'd like to hide from the prying eyes of other people and from God. I mean evidence that our very nature is so sinful that we don't even recognize the gravity of our problem. *Sin* is not a bunch of deeds that we can fix one sin at a time. *Sin* is a condition of our hearts that reveals itself through our behavior.

Handsful of Darkness

What can we do about sin? Well, nothing on our own. As Jeremiah said, it's something we can't remedy: "Can the Ethiopian change his skin or the leopard its spots? Neither can you do good who are accustomed to doing evil" (Jeremiah 13:23).

If you want to empty a room of darkness when the power's off, you don't grab handsful of darkness and throw them out of the room. You light a candle. The solution to sin in the life is to light the candle, not to focus on the darkness. As I mentioned before, dealing with sin is like dealing with a case of the measles. If, when you've got measles, your main concern is your appearance, you could apply makeup and hide your disease from other people. But if you really want to deal with the problem, then the spots wouldn't concern you so much as the disease itself. You wouldn't put your energy into covering up the spots with makeup, you'd focus on the rest, liquids, and medicine that can stop the course of the disease.

If sin is just an action or a behavior, then trying to fix it one act at a time makes sense. But if sin is a disease, we must attack that disease and not just the symptoms. Victory over *Sin* must come first. That will lead to victory over sinful behavior.

Defining the second word, "righteousness," makes this even clearer. Just as we tend to think of sin as mistakes we make or bad deeds that we need to eliminate, so we generally think of righteousness as doing good deeds and refraining from doing bad deeds. The rich young ruler who approached Jesus thought in similar terms. When he asked Jesus, " 'Good teacher, what must I do to inherit eternal life?' " (Luke 18:18), he was saying,

"I've done a lot of good already, but there must be at least one more thing You can think of that I can add to my lengthy list of good deeds."

We won't find the means to victory over sin—sanctification—in the discovery of some tool that will help us make character adjustments. It's not like going to a chiropractor for a back adjustment. Nor is it like scraping the barnacles off the hull of our essentially good self. God is not interested in tinkering with our lives. He's after something totally new.

So, where will we find victory? In transplanted hearts. God promises, "A new heart also will I give you, and a new spirit will I put within you: and I will take away the stony heart out of your flesh, and I will give you an heart of flesh" (Ezekiel 36:26, KJV). Faith in God, rather than rebellion against God, fills this new heart. That's an important part of the solution, for Paul says, "Everything that does not come from faith is sin" (Romans 14:23). If it doesn't come from faith, if it doesn't come from the transformed heart, it is sin.

Our focus should not be simply on getting rid of sinful behavior or on adding righteous deeds, but on building a faith relationship with Jesus. As Ellen White says:

> All true obedience comes from the heart. It was heart work with Christ. And if we consent, He will so identify Himself with our thoughts and aims, so blend our hearts and minds into conformity to His will, that when obeying Him we shall be but carrying out our own impulses. The will, refined and sanctified, will find its highest delight in doing His service. When we know God as it is our privilege to know Him, our life will be a life of continual obedience. Through an appreciation of the character of Christ, through communion with God, sin will become hateful to us. As Christ lived the law in humanity, so we may do if we will take hold of the Strong for strength. (*The Desire of Ages*, p. 668.)

Paul emphasizes the centrality to our sanctification of God's work in us. He wrote that Christ is both our righteousness and our sanctification, and he prayed for his converts, "May the God of peace Himself sanctify you wholly; and may your spirit and soul and body be kept sound and blameless at the coming of our Lord Jesus Christ. He who calls you is faithful, and he will do it" (1 Thessalonians 5:23, 24, RSV; cf. 1 Corinthians 1:30).

Believing that God exists and that the Bible is true, even believing that Jesus is God's Son and the Messiah who died so people could live, is not enough. God has called each of His sons and daughters to live a sanctified life: "Those who obey his commands live in him, and he in them. And this is how we know that he lives in us: We know it by the Spirit he gave us." "We know that we have come to know him if we obey his commands" (1 John 3:24; 2:3).

The good news is that God promises to help us live the life He wants us to live. Our part is to invite Him into our lives every moment of every day. Turn your thoughts to Him first thing in the morning. Thank Him for life, and then invite Him, through His Spirit, to take charge of your thoughts and words and feelings and deeds for the day.

Then, as you read His Word, note His promises: He "is able to keep you from falling and to present you before his glorious presence without fault and with great joy" (Jude 24). "The Lord is faithful; he will strengthen you and guard you from evil" (2 Thessalonians 3:3, RSV). Underline the texts that reveal the scope of our High Priest's ministry for us through the Holy Spirit.

Ask Jesus!

But you say, "I know I should do all these things, but I don't. I should wake up early and pray and study my Bible, but I don't. I should keep my eyes on Jesus, but I don't. What can I do?"

Ask Him! Ask Him to awaken you. Ask Him to make you want to follow Him. Ask Him to make you willing to keep your thoughts on Him. The apostle John wrote, "To all who received him, who believed in his name, he gave power to become children of God" (John 1:12, NRSV). He still does!

Once a woman wanted to clean her home, so she went to a store and bought all kinds of cleaning supplies. She bought dish soap, laundry soap, bathroom cleansers, brushes, towels, a broom, a mop, and just about every disinfectant she could find.

She cleaned, disinfected, soaked, and scrubbed everything in the house until it was as clean as she could make it. And she felt good—until one day her son came home with a huge magnifying glass that he had borrowed from a friend. Holding it up to a wall, he called, "Look at this, Mommy!" Through the magnifying glass, the woman saw that what looked clean to the naked eye was not so clean after all.

So this woman redoubled her efforts. In fact, she scrubbed some walls so thoroughly that she had to repaint them. But then the house looked and smelled so nice and clean that she really felt good—until one day her son came home from school with a microscope he had borrowed from the science lab. He brought into focus some of the dust he had discovered in a corner under a bed.

"Hey, Mom, look at this!"

The woman looked, and saw on the microscope's slide thousands of dust mites.

"Where did you get that?" she cried.

"Under your bed," the boy responded innocently.

"How can I keep the house clean if dust hides under the furniture?" the woman wailed. Then she sold all the furniture in her house. And taking bleach and disinfectant, she went over the whole house again. The house was as clean as she could make it. And it smelled like a hospital. But it was also empty—because the family couldn't live there without furniture. They had to move into an apartment down the street. So the house sat there—untouched, but clean.

At least the woman thought it was clean, until one day she stuck her head in just to feel what it was like to be in a clean house. Then she discovered that dust and dirt know no barriers. Though empty and unused, the house had continued to accumulate dust and dirt. It was dirtier than it had ever been.

That story reminds me of one of Jesus' parables: "When an evil spirit comes out of a man," He said, "it goes through arid places seeking rest and does not find it. Then it says, 'I will return to the house I left.' When it arrives, it finds the house unoccupied, swept clean and put in order. Then it goes and takes with it seven other spirits more wicked than itself, and they go in and live there. And the final condition of that man is worse than the first" (Matthew 12:43-45).

Only a person full of Jesus and clothed with the robe of His righteousness can be victorious. As Ellen White put it so beautifully:

> When we submit ourselves to Christ, the heart is united with His heart, the will is merged in His will, the mind becomes one with His mind, the thoughts are brought into captivity to Him; we live His life. . . . Then as the Lord looks upon us He sees, not the fig-leaf garment, not the nakedness and deformity of sin, but His own robe of righteousness, which is perfect obedience to the law of Jehovah. (*Christ's Object Lessons*, p. 311.)

Repentance, assurance, victory—what a glorious progression the Lord has provided for us! But all come only in Christ—we cannot generate them ourselves. In the next chapter we take another "in Christ" step as we hear God's call to compassion.

4

Called to Compassion— in Christ

Hurting with others.

We're shocked by the news we see on television:

■ In the Middle East, with the backdrop of a line of Kurdish women waiting for safe drinking water, a reporter narrates, "Recently, up to a thousand children a day died here, most of them from diseases related to contaminated water."

■ From Southern Asia a reporter announces, "A devastating cyclone ripped through Bangladesh, killing more than 139,000 and leaving 10 million homeless."

■ From Somalia, Ethiopia, and the Sudan we hear news of millions threatened with starvation.

■ In Peru, health officials estimate that recently more than 1,400 people died from cholera.

■ Worldwide, every minute of every day, eighteen children under the age of five die of hunger.

What happens to us when, day after day, we see, hear, and read about overwhelming suffering?

Visitors to the home of a prominent English author are shown the row of trees that he planted to shut out the view of the slaughterhouse next door. Like him, most of us desire to screen out things that bring us pain. We do whatever we can to insulate ourselves from the suffering of others. Overdoses of the world's suffering, particularly when combined with inaction on our part, can inoculate us against compassion.

Highway Accident

Kevin Ishmael had the hardening shell of his compassion broken by an accident on an interstate highway in Michigan. The sun was just beginning to lighten the sky when the call came over the radio of the charter bus he was driving: "Hey, anybody out there know first aid? There's a bad accident south of the South Haven exit. I'm going to need help."

Though Kevin had worked two years as a paramedic, he didn't want to stop. He was taking his passengers on a day trip to Chicago, and he knew that stopping at the accident scene could take an hour or two if things didn't go well. But when a quick glance at his watch revealed that they were ahead of schedule, he guided the bus to the shoulder of the road, grabbed his first-aid kit, and sprinted across the divided highway.

The car involved in the accident had smashed through a guard-rail, rolled a few times, and then landed upside down in the water of a drainage ditch. He could see two hands—definitely a woman's—under the demolished vehicle.

Kevin hurried over to a man who was extinguishing a fire on the car. He was the truck driver who had radioed for help. Kevin asked, "Did you try to get a pulse?"

"Yeah, but there's nothing. I'm afraid she didn't make it."

Stepping into the murky water, Kevin waded over to the body. He dropped to his knees, lifted an arm out of the water, and felt for some evidence of life.

"You're right," he said, shaking his head. "Too bad."

The truck driver remarked that he had radioed for an ambulance. "Yeah. Well, tell them not to hurry," Kevin responded.

Just then a young woman who had joined them said, "I think that's Leah Morris. We both work at the same factory."

A surge of adrenalin shot through Kevin, setting his arms and legs on fire and his heart pounding out of control. He jumped to his feet and grabbed the side of the car, while the truck driver gaped at him in surprise.

"Don't just stand there," Kevin shouted. "Help me! We've got to save her. Leah's under there . . . Leah Morris. She's my sister!"

The truck driver and Kevin seized the Buick Century. Like two characters in a slow-motion movie, they rolled it off Leah. Kevin dragged Leah's body out of the water and onto dry ground. Turning her over, he scooped the mud from her mouth and began cardiopulmonary resuscitation.

Breathe . . . Breathe . . . Push, two, three, four . . . thirteen, fourteen, fifteen. Kevin repeated the CPR routine over and over again—two full breaths, fifteen chest compressions. After a few minutes he checked for a pulse. "She's alive!" he yelled to the truck driver. "Tell the ambulance we need them here *fast.*"

When the ambulance arrived, Kevin helped the paramedics strap Leah to the stretcher and put her in the ambulance. He followed the ambulance to the hospital and followed again when she was transferred to a larger hospital, staying with her until she regained consciousness some nineteen hours later. Eventually, to Kevin's joy, Leah returned home to her husband and six-month-old daughter.

The experience made Kevin rethink his outlook on the misfortunes of others. He wrote: "I thank God for using me to save Leah's life. Yet a troubling thought . . . keeps running through my mind: What if Leah's co-worker had not been there to identify her? When I arrived at the scene of the accident, the woman under the car was just another highway statistic. How quickly my attitude changed when I found out she was my sister, a member of *my* family.

"If I've learned one thing from this experience," he continued, "it's the importance of valuing every human being. Even those whom society tends to ignore—ghetto children, prisoners, unwed mothers, homeless wanderers—are part of God's family. And since all of us are His children, every person I meet is my brother, my sister."[1]

As Kevin discovered, those who have found assurance and victory in Christ cannot go on living self-focused lives. They have been called to live lives of compassion.

The Father of Compassion

The Bible makes our calling clear in how it pictures our heavenly Father and in what it says about how He relates to all of the problems of the world. We might be tempted to think of Him as the Father of all discipline, the Father of all righteousness, the Father of all truth and justice. All these characterizations would be true, but they're not the picture Paul gives his converts in Corinth. In the opening words of his second letter to them, he calls God "the Father of compassion" (2 Corinthians 1:3).

Compassion means "to suffer or hurt with." Our God is the Father who *"hurts with."*

Jesus portrayed that compassion in His life:

■ He had compassion for the *lost*—"When he saw the crowds, he had compassion on them, because they were harassed and helpless, like sheep without a shepherd" (Matthew 9:36).

■ He had compassion for the *sick*—"When Jesus landed and saw a large crowd, he had compassion on them and healed their sick" (Matthew 14:14).

■ He had compassion for the *hungry*—"I have compassion for these people; they have already been with me three days and have nothing to eat" (Mark 8:2).

■ He had compassion for the *handicapped*—"Jesus had compassion on them and touched their eyes. Immediately they received their sight and followed him" (Matthew 20:34).

God has compassion. He "hurts with" people. The Incarnation—His coming to earth—illustrates His compassion, His "hurting with." When Adam and Eve turned from Him to sin, God didn't destroy them and begin a new creation. He "hurt with" them—with us! "Therefore the Lord himself will give you a sign: The virgin will be with child and will give birth to a son, and will call him Immanuel" (Isaiah 7:14). *Immanuel* means "God with us." God showed that He "hurt with" us by becoming a human and experiencing the pain. He didn't just make a phone call from heaven and say, "I'm awfully sorry about your problem!" He didn't just mail a nice note or card that said "Hope you get well soon!" God became human to hurt with us.

Paul's letter to the Corinthians continues: "Praise be to the God and Father of our Lord Jesus Christ, the Father of compassion and the God of all comfort, who comforts us in all our troubles, *so that* we can comfort those in any trouble with the comfort we ourselves have received from God" (2 Corinthians 1:3, 4, emphasis supplied). You see, there's a purpose to God's hurting with us. He comforts us in our troubles *so that* we can comfort others in trouble. As He has compassion, so we are to have compassion. God doesn't comfort us to make us *comfortable*, but to make us *comforters*.

Peter tells us the same thing: "Be ye all of one mind, having compassion one of another" (1 Peter 3:8, KJV). John says it too, but he uses a different word: "Beloved, let us love one another" (1 John 4:7, KJV). And in another text, Paul repeats it:

> If you have any encouragement from being united with Christ, if any comfort from his love, if any fellowship with the Spirit, if any tenderness and compassion, then make my joy complete by being like-minded, having the same love, being one in spirit and purpose. Do nothing out of selfish ambition or vain conceit, but in humility consider others better than yourselves. Each of you should look not only to your own interests, but also to the interests of others. (Philippians 2:1-4.)

A Shoulder to Lean On

Can you imagine the heaven-like atmosphere God intends His earthly family to enjoy—a place where love for others is the guiding principle, where each person is more interested in the well-being and happiness of others than his own? In the world as God wishes it, peace born of unselfishness would replace harsh words and lonely hearts. People would never have to bear a burden alone. Everyone would have a shoulder to lean on. And eternity would loom bright in joyful anticipation of being with God, the world's best Friend.

Those who have become citizens of His kingdom should do their best to see God's plans fulfilled now. And many are. Whenever I think of compassion and understanding, I think of my aunt Mary Green, a dedicated Bible instructor who worked with two pastors—my father and Sunny Liu—for some years in New York and California. Aunt Mary didn't keep track of how many hours she put in, especially when there was someone she could share with—whether it was friendship, a home-cooked meal, a Bible study, her home, or simply lending her ear to someone who was hurting. Her multiplied sorrows enabled her to comfort all, because she had been there before. I never had the privilege of sitting in on one of her Bible studies. But I knew what she believed—I saw her live it.

Aunt Mary died before she retired. I'm sure God decided she deserved to rest. During the last year of her life she saw forty people with whom she had studied reborn spiritually. She kept going when her pain was so severe that others had to drive her from home to home. Her last whispered words were, "I know whom I have believed." And we knew too. Everything about her showed she knew and loved Him and all of His earthly children, erring or not. It is to such "other-mindedness" that God calls each of us.

There are those who are answering His call. Take Queenie Brodie, for instance. In 1971, Ronald Reagan, then governor of California, inaugurated an experimental program called Match-Two. The program involves enlisting volunteers from the community to befriend prison inmates who have no friends. The volunteers visit the prisoners monthly, correspond with them between visits, and help them make the transition back to society upon their release.

One Sabbath morning early in 1991, Debbie Schmidt, regional director of the Match-Two program, stood before a Camarillo, California, congregation and held out a handful of applications from young people, ages thirteen to twenty-five, who desperately needed a friend. Most of them hadn't had a visitor since they entered prison.

Queenie and Bill Brodie each selected an application from Debbie's notebook. Then Queenie asked, "What about the rest of these kids?"

Debbie replied, "I have no one for them. I was lucky today—I got four matches from your church. Many times I go to churches and no one responds."

As Queenie and Bill met with their kids, they became increasingly convinced that they had done the right thing. But the other pages in Debbie's book kept haunting Queenie. One day as she was returning from the prison, she stopped at a market. Happening upon a friend from church, she—with characteristic enthusiasm—began telling her about the prisoner she was visiting. As Queenie concluded, she added, "This is something you really ought to do!"

When her friend agreed to give it a try, Queenie thought *Wow! That was easy. I think I'll ask some more.* Getting on the phone, she began calling people she believed would be receptive to the idea. When she finished going through her church list, she began visiting neighboring churches. She figures she's involved at least one hundred people.[2]

Then there's Karen Kotoske. On a trip to the back country of Mexico, Karen, a dental hygienist from northern California, saw the desperate need of the Huichol Indians. Since they live in an area where they can't count on receiving adequate water, their harvests often fail. The resultant hunger leads to malnutrition and disease.

Moved by compassion, Karen established a foundation that not only supplies food in times of need but helps the Huichol develop dependable water supplies. She accepted the need she saw as God's personal call to service.[3]

And Roger and Shari Weis: When they married, they determined to do something to benefit society. At first they thought of the Peace Corps. But then they noticed the problems that surrounded them right where they lived. Now they care for foster children the Child Protective Services calls "habilitative." That means children with special needs, many suffering the effects of their parents' drug use. To enable them to carry on this ministry, both Shari and Roger work part time and split the care of the children fifty-fifty.

Roger says, "When [Child Protective Services] brings a child with drug-related problems, I feel this enormous amount of fury at the avoidable tragedy. Then somehow I find it in myself to let go of the rage. These kids need my compassion, not my anger. I *know* how it hurts to see children like this, but when people choose to not get involved and to look the other way, it makes the problem greater.

"Not everyone can be a foster parent, but if everyone would help just a little, we could make a difference."[4]

Like an Overflowing Cup

But suppose compassion doesn't come naturally or easily to us?

Paul has some answers. He doesn't just tell us that we should have compassion. He tells us how we can develop this godly trait: "For just as the sufferings of Christ flow over into our lives, so also through Christ our comfort overflows" (2 Corinthians 1:5). Picture a cup so full that it overflows onto the ground. In the same way our lives can become so full of the comfort that God gives us that our compassion will spill over to all around us. Then we'll hurt with others—and, as we share in their pain, we'll bring them with us when we go to God for comfort.

"But," perhaps you're saying, "I don't like pain; I don't like to hurt." Maybe you're one of those who turn off the television when the screen fills with pictures of the bloated bellies of malnourished children. "Life is tough enough," you say. "Why should I expose myself to more pain?"

Paul tells us why: "I want to know Christ . . . and the fellowship of sharing in his sufferings, becoming like him in his death" (Philippians 3:10). Paul wasn't a masochist who sought out pain for pain's sake. He says he wants to know Christ. Paul was aware that knowing Christ requires "fellowshipping" in His sufferings. That means more than just thinking about the pain He suffered on the cross. Fellowshipping with Christ's sufferings means identifying with others in their pain as He identified with us in ours. To know Christ is to identify with others as He identified with us. To identify with others is to identify with Him. "Inasmuch as ye have done it unto one of the least of these my brethren, ye have done it unto me" (Matthew 25:40, KJV).

"But we're compassionate," you reply. "We try to help others."

Yes, but we often prefer to be selective with our compassion:

■ We have compassion for people with AIDS—as long as they got the disease from a blood transfusion.

■ We have compassion for people who've lost their jobs—as long as it wasn't their fault.

■ We have compassion for people whose houses burn down—as long as they didn't start the fire by smoking in bed.

In other words, we have compassion for the *deserving*. But what must one be to be considered deserving? Isn't it enough to be hungry? Isn't it enough to be thirsty? Isn't it enough to be in prison? As sinners we have all received God's compassion. Were we *deserving* sinners? Are there some sinners for whom God feels no compassion—some He considers undeserving?

Compassion for the deserving frequently isn't compassion at all, but rather a reward for good behavior. The compassion that reflects Christ's example is the expression of empathetic feeling for the undeserving, just as Christ's death was for the undeserving—for you and for me.

Once a boy was swimming in a river. He got out too far and was in danger of drowning. A man who was walking along a road beside the river heard the boy's cries for help and began scolding the boy for being so careless and getting into deep water. But he made no attempt to help the boy.

"Oh, sir," cried the boy. "Please help me first! Scold me later!"

The needy of the world get plenty of scolding. Rather than scolding, they need compassion—someone who will help them. Yet so often we're tempted to think, if not to say, *Well, they wouldn't suffer so much if they had acted differently.*

It's true that we have to make decisions, often some pretty difficult ones. Maybe we can't be so generous with the first needy person who comes our way that we're left with nothing for others who may have even greater needs. But though we must make difficult choices, that's no reason to conclude that we can't help anyone!

When television overwhelms me with images of need, I can choose to do something, somewhere, or I can use the overload as an excuse to do nothing. I can choose to exercise compassion on at least a small part of the world, or I can fold my arms and say the problems are too big. Compassion is not sentimental sadness over anonymous suffering multitudes. It is specific action for specific need. Compassion means to hurt with someone else.

What Can I Do?

A boy walked along a beach with his father the morning after a tremendous storm. The huge waves the storm had raised had stranded thousands of starfish on the shore. Now they were dying.

As the two moved along the beach, the boy picked up one starfish after another and flung them back into the ocean. His father, looking down the miles of beach at the thousands of stranded starfish, said, "Why are you wasting your energy? Look at all of them. What possible difference can you make?"

"It makes a big difference to this one," the boy said as he picked up another starfish, looked at it, and threw it into the sea.

Someone once asked Mother Teresa a question similar to that father's. How could she and the few who were helping her hope to make an impact on Calcutta's three thousand slums—slums into which additional multitudes were pouring daily? She replied, "I do not think the way you think. I do not add. I only subtract from the total dying."

We must have compassion—no matter how futile our little efforts may appear. We must have compassion—not just for the deserving, but for the needy. In the day of judgment, it's not church attendance or church membership that will distinguish the righteous from the wicked. As the Bible tells us, it's compassion:

> Then the King will say to those on his right, "Come, you
> who are blessed by my Father; take your inheritance, the
> kingdom prepared for you since the creation of the world.
> For I was hungry and you gave me something to eat, I was

thirsty and you gave me something to drink, I was a stranger and you invited me in, I needed clothes and you clothed me, I was sick and you looked after me, I was in prison and you came to visit me" (Matthew 25:34-36).

Jesus "hurt with us"—and so, as His children, we ought to hurt with others. We ought to have compassion. As we touch others, we touch God. In that sense, Clement of Alexandria was right when he said, "If thou hast seen thy brother, thou hast seen God." His words reflect those of Jesus: "I tell you the truth, whatever you did for one of the least of these brothers of mine, you did for me" (Matthew 25:40).

Dr. Brand, who worked for eighteen years at Christian Medical College in Vellore, India, tells the following story about one of his patients—Sadan, a victim of leprosy. After four years of reconstructive surgery and rehabilitation therapy, Sadan was doing well enough to return home to his family for a weekend. "I want to go back to where I was rejected," he said proudly, referring to the cafes that had turned him away and the buses that had denied him service.

Before Sadan left, he and the doctor reviewed the dangers his trip would pose. Leprosy destroys the nerves that enable a person to feel pain. Because of this, its victims often are not aware of sharp, hot, or abrasive objects that are injuring them. Such injuries pose great threats to their bodies. Dr. Brand reminded Sadan of this fact and warned him to be careful of situations in which such injuries could occur.

Back home, Sadan ate a reunion dinner with his family on Saturday night. Then he went to his room. He hadn't slept there for four years. Just lying there was a great comfort. At last he was home!

The next morning Sadan examined himself as he had been trained to do at the hospital. To his horror, he found that the back of his left index finger had been mangled. Sadan knew the culprit. A rat had visited him during the night and gnawed his finger.

He thought of returning to the hospital, but decided to continue his visit one more day. Determined to stay awake so no rats would bother him, he set out to read through the night. But by 4:00 a.m., Sadan could no longer fight sleep. As he dozed off, his hand slid against the hot glass of the kerosene lamp by which he had been reading. By the time he awoke the next morning, a large patch of skin on the back of his right hand had been seriously burned.

Sadan returned to the hospital at Vellore the next day. As Dr. Brand removed the bandages, Sadan wept and said, "I feel as if I've lost all my freedom." And then he asked a significant question: "How can I be free without pain?"

Pain unites the different parts of our bodies in a network of communication. People who are close to each other share pain and joy even though no nerves connect them physically. They hurt with one another.

The world in which we live is a community. By creation and redemption, all of us who live on this earth are children of God—and brothers and sisters of one another: "And he [God] made from one every nation of men to live on all the face of the earth" (Acts 17:26, RSV). It is by our compassion, the willingness "to hurt with" each other, that we show that we know our Creator.

This compassion comes from Jesus. When we are in Him, we see as He sees and feel as He feels. Just as the Lord calls us to repentance, assurance, and victory in Christ, so He calls us to Christ's compassion.

In the next chapter we will explore another step in Christian living—the call to witness.

---

[1]Kevin Morris as told to Renee Coffee, "Rescue on Interstate 196," *Signs of the Times*, March 1992, page 19.

[2]Jeannette Johnson tells the story in *Paint the World With Love—Second Coat* (Hagerstown, MD: Review and Herald Publishing Association, 1992), pages 34-43.

[3]See Kit Watts, "A Place I Can Serve," *Signs of the Times*, February 1993, pages 16-19.

[4]See Christie Craig, "Little Victims, Big Hearts," *Signs of the Times*, September 1992, pages 16-18.

5

Called to Witness— in Christ

More than duty—a joy.

Building the Golden Gate Bridge between San Francisco and the Marin peninsula was a dangerous proposition. By the time construction had reached the half-way mark, twenty workers had suffered falls that resulted in serious injury or death. Dissatisfaction with this casualty rate led supervisors to stop work on the bridge until a giant net had been added under the construction area to catch anyone who fell. During the rest of the work on the project, only eight men fell. The net not only increased the workers' safety but it also made them more confident and so less likely to fall. In addition, their efficiency improved by 25 percent! Their confidence increased their productivity.

With the assurances we have of God's grace and care, we can experience a similar confidence in our spiritual lives. And like those workmen on the Golden Gate Bridge, when we have that assurance, that confidence, we also will be more productive.

In what ways are Christians to be productive?

After the resurrection, in what is called the Great Commission, Jesus assigned a task to those who believe in Him: "Therefore go and make disciples of all nations, baptizing them in the name of the Father and of the Son and of the Holy Spirit, and teaching them to obey everything I have commanded you. And surely I am with you always, to the very end of the age" (Matthew 28:19, 20).

Soon after, on the very day He ascended to heaven, Jesus reminded His disciples of this mission: "You will be my witnesses in Jerusalem, and in all Judea and Samaria, and to the ends of the earth" (Acts 1:8).

So Jesus today still commissions His disciples—those who have experienced His power to save—to tell others what He offers and to make disciples of them. The church is a community of believers whose lives are being transformed by the Holy Spirit. It is God's church only as the lives of its members experience and demonstrate the faith of Jesus. Witness is the reason the church exists. At its best, the church is a community of Christians who care deeply for one another and invite others to share in the peace of assurance in Christ and the joy of the family of God.

End-time Witnesses

The Bible clearly portrays such a role for the church—particularly in what it calls the "time of the end," the time just before Jesus returns to earth to end the problems of sin and pain and death once and for all. The prophecies of Daniel and Revelation accurately foretell the major events of world history. They indicate that the church established after Jesus' first advent would suffer intense persecution and then go into a 1,260-year-long decline, during which much of the truth about God that Jesus had brought would be subverted by false teachings (see Revelation 1-3 and 2 Thessalonians 2:1-12).

Using a woman to symbolize the church Jesus established, Revelation focuses attention on what it calls the "remnant of her seed" (chapter 12:17, KJV). A *remnant* is what remains. A remnant of fabric isn't any different than what came from the bolt of material earlier. It's the same thing, distinguished from the rest only by being the last of it—what comes at the end. The woman's "seed" are her children. So the "remnant of her seed" are the last "children" or members of the church—those living at the end of time, just before Jesus returns.

Revelation indicates this remnant has a specific task. It's to help prepare people for Jesus' second coming, to preach the everlasting gospel—the good news about getting right with God. We are living in the time of the remnant. The prophetic sections of the Bible make this clear. The "time of the end" indicated by its time prophecies has come. The "signs" in the sun, moon, and stars Jesus and the prophets said would tell us when the end is near have already taken place. Jesus' coming can't be far off.

So where are the members of the remnant? *Who* are they? Revelation offers a description of these people. They are "those who keep the commandments of God and have the testimony of Jesus" (Revelation 12:17, KJV). Chapter 14:12 adds that they "have the faith of Jesus."

The phrase "keep the commandments of God" is easy enough to understand. Obviously, the remnant take seriously what God has said, the direction He gives people's lives through His word—including, certainly, the Ten Commandments. Revelation 19:10 and 22:8, 9 make it clear that "the testimony of Jesus" involves the Holy Spirit working in people's lives through the gift of prophecy. And "the faith of Jesus" refers to the gospel He proclaimed, a gospel that says, "For God so loved the world that He gave His one and only Son, that *whoever believes in Him shall not perish but have eternal life*" (John 3:16, emphasis supplied).

I believe the Seventh-day Adventist church was called into existence specifically to do the work of the remnant. It arose at the right time in God's prophetic timetable. And it has the characteristics Revelation specifies: it preaches the faith of Jesus (Revelation 14:6's "eternal gospel") and the commandments of God (among them, the fourth commandment, the seventh-day Sabbath). And the gift of prophecy played a major role in founding the church and gives it direction even today.

In addition, the Seventh-day Adventist church actively attempts to fulfill Jesus' commission to preach the gospel in all the world to every creature in preparation for His second advent. As of December 31, 1992, the Seventh-day Adventist church's mission program encompassed 204 of the 233 nations recognized by the United Nations. In addition, in 1990, the church began an outreach drive called Global Mission. This drive aims by the year 2000 to establish congregations in each of the world's population groups of more than a million that have not yet heard the full gospel.

The church's outreach takes many forms: its 5,551 educational institutions, which include primary- through university-level schools, teach the three Rs in the larger setting of what it means to be a Christian. Following Jesus' example in using the restoration of physical health as a first step toward the restoration of spiritual well-being, the church also operates various types of medical facilities around the world—including 161 hospitals and sanitariums, 340 clinics and dispensaries, and fifty-seven medical launches and airplanes that serve remote areas.

And of course, worldwide the church uses the communications media, operating fifty-seven publishing houses, that produce 295 periodicals in 190 languages, and originate programs that run weekly on more than 2,000 television stations and 4,000 radio stations (some of which it owns and operates). The church uses the spoken word in another 687 languages and dialects.

A Personal Privilege

But the church is composed of individuals. And the commission to witness wasn't given just to the church as an organization—or even to some members of the church supposed to be especially suited to the task. Jesus has given this commission to every disciple of His. It's a personal call to a personal responsibility. More than that, it's a privilege extended to everyone who has accepted salvation from Him. "Come, follow me," Jesus said, "and I will make you fishers of men" (Matthew 4:19). Could the converse be true too, that if we are not fishers of men, then we are not really following Him?

Consider this riddle about frogs: "If there were five frogs on a log and one decided to jump, how many would be left on the log?" The answer to the riddle is five, because deciding to jump is not the same as jumping. Being called to witness by Christ is not the same as being a witness.

How do we become true Christian witnesses? We tend to think of witnessing as leaving a piece of gospel literature somewhere or occasionally inviting someone to attend some meetings in which the gospel is preached. But witnessing is more inclusive than that. Its nature is revealed by how Jesus communicated with us. God wanted to witness to us about the good news of the birth of His Son and the eternal life that was ours if we would accept it. He wanted to tell us the truth about His own and His Son's character. He didn't do it just by sending us literature—the Bible. God sent His Son, Jesus, in person so we could experience how loving and unselfish He really is.

When the authorities ordered Peter and John not to talk about Jesus anymore, they replied: "We cannot help speaking about what we have seen and heard" (Acts 4:20). Witnessing is like that. It shouldn't be something we have to force ourselves to do. Nor is it like a requirement, a special "work" that contributes to our salvation. Instead, when we love Jesus and enjoy the assurance of salvation, we can't help speaking about Him.

John wrote, "But as many as received him, to them gave he power to become the sons of God, even to them that believe on his name" (John 1:12, KJV). When we've experienced that power, that change, then the joy of assurance in Christ will give birth to witness. Then we'll see all around us opportunities for witness. We'll not have to look for a good place to carry out this task. We'll recognize that the best place to witness is the place where we spend most of our time.

When, some years ago, the message of assurance in Christ moved from theory to reality in my life—from my head to my heart—I found my whole approach to witnessing changed. It was no longer an unnatural effort motivated by some new promotion or program. Whenever I found myself with other people, I couldn't help but witness to my joy in Jesus.

That's what God wants witness to be—not some task, some duty, we faithfully but dourly fulfill. Rather, He wants so to live in us by the Holy Spirit that other people can see the joy we've gained by being followers of Jesus. Wrote Ellen White:

The true Christian draws his motives for action from his deep love for his Redeemer. His affection for his Master is true and holy. And it is the cheerful, lovable Christian of whom Christ says, "Ye are my witnesses" (Isaiah 43:10). Such a man is Christ's representative, for he reflects Christ in his daily life. It is when he recedes from the light that he cannot diffuse its bright beams to others. (*The Youth's Instructor*, March 24, 1898.)

The closer we are to Jesus, the more we will reflect Him in our lives. As we experience victory and assurance, we will attract others to Him.

How Shall We Witness?

And how shall we witness? Personal testimony is the most effective and convincing way to witness. We need to tell what we know, what we've seen and heard and felt. If we've been following Jesus step by step, we'll have something to say concerning the way He's led us. We'll be able to tell how we've tested His promises and found them true. We'll be able to bear witness to what we've known of the grace of Christ.

When Christians speak from personal experience about the meaning Christianity has given their lives, and when their lives back up their words, their argument in favor of Christianity becomes compelling. While people can reject such testimony, they can't dismiss it or ignore it. It calls for a decision of some sort.

The Bible is filled with powerful personal testimonies of this kind. When officers apprehended Jesus, they were forced to admit, "Never man spake like this man" (John 7:46, KJV). At the cross, the centurion recognized, "Truly this was the Son of God" (Matthew 27:54, KJV). And on seeing the risen Christ, Thomas, who had doubted the resurrection, confessed, "My Lord and my God" (John 20:28, KJV). Think also of the other examples of personal testimony: the changed demoniacs telling what Jesus had done for them; the witness of Lazarus returned from the dead; Mary, changed from mourner to enthusiast when she saw the resurrected Christ; and Paul's unflagging testimony, "I am not ashamed: for I know whom I have believed" (2 Timothy 1:12, KJV).

Personal testimonies such as these fueled the growth of the early church. The confirmation of these testimonies in the hearts of believers today is the foundation of life-witness.

After all, personal, firsthand information is the hallmark of a witness. Witnessing can't be done by proxy. You can't pay someone else to do it for you. A witness is someone who's been there, who's seen something for himself or herself, who's now testifying about the experience. As John wrote, "That which was from the beginning, *which we have heard, which we have seen with our eyes, which we have looked at and our hands have touched—this we proclaim* concerning the Word of life. The life appeared; we have seen it and testify to it, and we proclaim to you the eternal life, which was with the Father and has appeared to us. We proclaim to you what we have seen and heard, so that you also may have fellowship with us" (1 John 1:1-3, emphasis supplied).

John's testimony of his personal experience gives me confidence in the truth of the gospel. We aren't following "cunningly devised fables" (2 Peter 1:16, KJV). John wasn't merely recording some tradition or jotting down rumors he'd heard. In his letters and Gospel, he wrote about what he *knew* to have happened—because he had experienced it. This is what makes what he wrote so powerful.

In contrast, think of the political advertisements you hear on the radio during election campaigns. Someone will deliver, in strong, authoritative tones, a passionate plea for your support of some political figure. You'd almost think the speaker believes the fate of the universe rests on the election of this individual. Then, as the story concludes, the same announcer tells listeners that what's been said was a paid advertisement and not necessarily the views of the station. Testimony loses its impact when you realize it doesn't really represent the speaker's convictions, that it's just words he or she has been paid to say.

Just as it was John's personal experience with Christ that makes his testimony compelling, so our testimony can only be compelling if it comes from our own experience with Jesus. We can't share what we don't have. To put it another way: what we share, we must not only believe but have also experienced. Personal experience places truth in a setting that enhances its credibility and power. Unless and until we possess a faith of our own, until we enjoy a trusting, intimate relationship with our Saviour, our proclamation of the gospel will sound superficial.

Our Testimony

And what shall we testify of? When we try to mold the opinions of people by presenting doctrines, the theory of truth, before those people know us personally, we run the danger of inoculating them against the gospel. Regardless of the truth of our doctrines, when they're presented apart from a personal testimony of our assurance in Christ, they seem cold, powerless, and theoretical. We need to approach people with caring, loving friendship, sharing our personal experience with God. Then the Holy Spirit can work on their hearts and minds.

Ellen White pointed out: "Christ's method alone will give true success in reaching the people. The Saviour mingled with men as one who desired their good. He showed His sympathy for them, ministered to their needs, and won their confidence. Then He bade them, 'Follow Me.' " (*The Ministry of Healing*, p. 143.)

We know others through relationships, so we best witness to them through those relationships. We witness best to those we know the best. If a stranger came to your door and asked to borrow fifty dollars, you probably would not lend the money. If, on the other hand, a close friend came to your door and made the same request, you would, because of your friendship, be much more inclined to respond positively. Likewise, our most effective influence for Jesus is with our closest friends.

Christian witnessing doesn't just happen on weekends or in evangelistic meetings. What happens during the week does more to spread the gospel than what happens during church services or on special occasions. And, as we've noted previously, this task is not reserved for the professionals: ministers and evangelists. Only a few people, relatively speaking, can enter full-time church employment, and they're not even the best ones to touch the lives of people outside the church. People who regularly come in contact with others at work, in their families, and in their neighborhoods are most effective at witnessing to them.

We all need to think of our vocations as locations for the

practice of our ministry. When our relationship with the Lord is what it should be, we'll be able to share our faith in the natural environment of work.

Does the call to witness scare you? Does Jesus' commission to take His gospel to all the world, to every "creature" in the world seem impossible to fulfill? Imagine how impossible it must have seemed to the disciples to whom He first gave it—a group of poorly educated men with little experience and few financial resources! But Jesus knows our needs. On the day of His ascension, He promised all His followers help in fulfilling the task He had assigned. He said He would send the Holy Spirit, who would bring power for witnessing. The results on the day of Pentecost, the day that promise began to be fulfilled, show just how effective the Holy Spirit's aid is. The witnessing done on that day resulted in three thousand accessions to the small group of Christian believers.

Jesus' promise of the Spirit's aid is as surely ours as is His commission. Each of us who becomes a follower of Jesus Christ— lay members as well as clergy—receives gifts from the Spirit, gifts to be used for the good of the church. According to Romans 12, 1 Corinthians 12, and Ephesians 4 these gifts include: serving, teaching, encouraging, contributing, leading, governing, showing mercy, and healing. They're not meant simply to enrich us or the churches to which we belong. They're meant to enable us to carry out Jesus' commission (see 1 Peter 4:10). In other words, whatever our gifts, we're to use them to witness, to lead others to Jesus and the salvation He offers.

How can we know what gifts we've received? Well, they generally lie along the lines of our natural abilities. But to discover them, we begin by making sure we're right with God and that our aim is to build His kingdom and not our own. Then we must study what the Bible has to say about the gifts, watch for the opportunities to serve that God sends your way, and seek the counsel of the body of believers—the church through which the gifts are to operate.

So Jesus has given us a big task. But it's not an impossible task—because He's also given us the means of fulfilling it.

The Shipwreck

Some years ago there was a shipwreck off the coast of the Pacific Northwest of North America. Huge waves pounded the unfortunate ship that had run aground. In a village near the site of the wreck, a crowd of fishermen gathered to watch as the men who manned the local life-saving station raced out to rescue those on board. After a terrific struggle, the rescuers came back with all the shipwrecked sailors but one. "There was no room in the lifeboat for him, so we told him to stay by the ship and someone would come back for him," shouted a young man. "Who will go with me?"

A youth raised his hand and then stepped toward the young man. As he did so, a woman cried out, "Don't go, Jim! Don't go! You are all I have left. Your father was drowned in the sea. Your brother William sailed away, and we've never heard from him. And if you are lost, I'll be left alone. Oh, Jim, please don't go!"

Jim listened to his mother's pleading, but then turned toward the raging sea and said, "Mother, I must go! It is my duty! I must go!"

The onlookers watched as the men in the lifeboat fought their way toward the wreck. Anxiously Jim's mother wept and prayed. Then the boat started back, a frail little shell tossed about by the angry waves. When it drew near, the people shouted, "Did you get him?"

Jim shouted back, "Yes! And tell Mother it's William!"

Throughout the world today there are Seventh-day Adventists rejoicing in their assurance of salvation and victory in Christ who are fulfilling the commission that Jesus gave His disciples. I think of one young man in a country I won't name who went to an area where the church had no presence. He raised up a body of believers amid terrifying persecution. In the process he was beaten, the place of worship burned, and his life repeatedly threatened. And yet today, the hope brought by the message of Christ's soon return shines in that community.

I think of the twenty-four young Seventh-day Adventist taskforce workers in predominantly Muslim Sudan who are laboring to bring Christ to the inhabitants of twelve cities. Their reports are exciting: fifteen baptized here, thirty-four baptized there, six Bible studies started in another place. And their stories reveal how the Lord has given them outstanding courage in the face of want and danger. One reports: "Even though gathered under a rented plastic tarp, the twenty-six new members still come faithfully." Another writes: "Between us, my evangelism partner and I have a pair of shoes and a pair of slippers. Whoever gives Bible studies in the village nine kilometers away gets to wear the shoes."

Rented tarps and insufficient clothing—yet the Holy Spirit is working through their efforts!

I think also of the student teams at our church's Spicer College in India. I've read many of their reports. Some of these young men and women walk ten, fifteen, twenty miles a day to bear witness in towns that until recently hadn't heard God's message for these last days of earth's history. Why do they walk? Because they don't have the money to buy bicycles. Their lack doesn't stop them. They go on undaunted. Spicer's New Mission Generation—students who daily count it a privilege to be ambassadors for Christ in their homeland—have already formed ninety-one new congregations.

But it's not just those who live in some foreign land who are called to witness. We all have prime opportunities for evangelism in our homes, our communities, and our workplaces. The lives of many of the people with whom you come into contact every day are in eternal jeopardy. These people are all children of God, and many of them need to hear from the lips of a friend the good news about Jesus. As Jim said as he went to rescue the last shipwrecked sailor, it's our duty.

It *is* the Christian's duty. But more than that, it is the Christian's *privilege* to rescue others for God and to know the joy of the angels, who rejoice over each sinner who repents.

Our study has taken us through five steps: repentance, assurance, victory, compassion, and witness. Let's remember that we don't take these steps on our own. They are always taken in Christ. In the next chapter we look at another part of the Christian life—the joyful expectancy of Christ's return.

6

Called to Expectancy— in Christ

How to wait for His return.

On New Year's Eve of 999 A.D., a mass of weeping worshipers gathered in the old basilica of St. Peter's in Rome. It was the end of the millennium and, they thought, perhaps also of the world. Many of these people had given away their homes and lands in an attempt to obtain for themselves forgiveness and vindication in the judgment they thought they would soon face.

People of the Middle Ages aren't the only ones who have feared they might personally greet the end of the world. In 1978 John Strong led a group of one hundred city dwellers to the Australian bush. They were hoping to escape the nuclear holocaust they believed would destroy the world on October 31. In 1992, a Korean preacher and his followers published advertisements in newspapers throughout Australia, South Korea, and North America warning that Christ would return on October 28 of that year. Later he was arrested, and Korean authorities charged him with financially defrauding his followers.

But the end of the world isn't just an interest of people on the fringes of society. For almost 2,000 years, through the highs and

65

lows of history, through the Middle Ages and the Reformation, Christians have meditated on, spoken of, and looked for the fulfillment of the promise of our Lord: "I will come again, and receive you unto myself; that where I am, there ye may be also" (John 14:3, KJV).

The Blessed Hope

Why have Christians considered belief in Jesus' return important?

The reason is that the Bible talks a lot about that event:

■ "For the Son of man shall come in the glory of his Father with his angels" (Matthew 16:27, KJV).

■ "And then shall they see the Son of man coming in a cloud with power and great glory" (Luke 21:27, KJV).

■ "If I go . . . , I will come again" (John 14:3, KJV).

■ "This same Jesus . . . shall so come in like manner as ye have seen him go into heaven" (Acts 1:11, KJV).

■ "Unto them that look for him shall he appear the second time without sin unto salvation" (Hebrews 9:28, KJV).

■ "Be ye also patient; . . . for the coming of the Lord draweth nigh" (James 5:8).

■ "Behold, he cometh with clouds; and every eye shall see him, and they also which pierced him" (Revelation 1:7, KJV).

Many of Jesus' parables and much of His message centered on His return. In fact, this teaching forms one of the major themes of the New Testament.

Paul called the prospect of Jesus' advent the "blessed hope" (Titus 2:13). As we see why it's the blessed hope, we also see why it's such a prominent theme in the Bible. The reason: The promises God has made to those who place their faith in Him—resurrection and eternal life; face-to-face communion with Him; reunion with our loved ones; the end of sickness, pain, sorrow, and death; and the restoration of the perfect creation He originally intended—all these are tied to and, in fact, dependent on this event.

Contrary to what many suppose, we don't go to our reward—heaven or hell—immediately upon death. Jesus linked the giving of rewards with His return: "Behold, I am coming soon! My reward is with me, and I will give to everyone according to what he has done" (Revelation 22:12).

Paul explains that at Jesus' coming all will be made alive and that believers will become immortal (see 1 Corinthians 15:22, 23, 51-53). His converts in Thessalonica apparently feared that those who died before the Lord returned were gone forever. Paul assured them that wasn't so. He told them it was Christ's advent that would make the difference: when Jesus comes, the dead will be raised, and both the dead and the living will be caught up to meet Him in the clouds. Then we all will be with the Lord—and each other—forever (see 1 Thessalonians 4:13-17).

It's when Jesus returns that God will make His home with the human race; that's when "He will wipe every tear from their eyes. There will be no more death or mourning or crying or pain, for the old order of things has passed away" (Revelation 21:4).

Maybe we can understand how vital it is to believe that Christ is coming by considering the implications of His never returning. That would make meaningless many of the messages He gave while He was here. For God to have come and healed the physical pain of a few people during one brief moment in history and then left forever makes no sense. That would be like a doctor giving a short-term painkiller to someone suffering from a curable disease and then leaving, never to return. Christ's first coming would be meaningless were there no second coming. Of what benefit would His forgiveness be? Of what use is the cross if there were to be no crown?

We wouldn't consider a God who would intervene for an instant of earth's history and then leave forever a loving God. Of that God we would have to ask, "Why did He come at all? Was He trying to increase our misery and pain by relieving it for a moment so we could understand how bad off we are?"

No, even if Jesus had not told us He was coming back, we

would know He was. The very concept of salvation implies a resurrection at His return.

If we want to know the hope the second coming offers, we only have to reflect on what His first coming meant. What Planet Earth experienced for a brief moment in history two thousand years ago, it will experience again. The promise of the second coming brings hope and joy because it says we will live again with Jesus, the same Jesus who lived among us, the same Jesus who loved, and comforted, and healed, and raised the dead. He is coming to be with us again.

Avoid the Deception

As we've seen earlier in this book, there's an adversary, someone who has opposed all that God has done and is doing for human beings. Since the second advent offers believers such hope and since it forms such an important part of God's plan for saving people, you might expect Satan, God's adversary, to attempt to disrupt it or to distract people from it.

In the instructions Jesus gave about the end of the world, He warned that false Christs would come "to deceive even the elect—if that were possible" (Matthew 24:24). Then He pointed out the signs that would mark the time of His coming and gave a brief description of His coming—some of its characteristics—so we could avoid the deception.

If a newspaper assigned us to write a news story concerning what the Bible has to say about the second coming, we'd begin by asking the questions reporters ask: *who, what, when, where, why,* and *how?* Let's ask these questions about the second coming.

Who is this story about? Jesus—"this same Jesus" (Acts 1:11), the Jesus the disciples knew, their Friend, Jesus of Nazareth, the One who was born in a stable, ministered in Judea, was crucified for our sins, resurrected, and ascended to heaven—and people. In fact, it's about every human being who has ever lived. At Jesus' return the angels gather His people, living and dead. And the events initiated at His coming move toward a time when everyone stands before God's throne (see Matthew 24:31; 1 Thessalonians 4:16, 17; Revelation 20:12-15).

What will happen? Christ this time will come as king rather than servant. His coming begins a new phase of the judgment (see Jude 14, 15; Revelation 22:12). It marks the change between the world as we know it and the new earth God will create to replace it (see 2 Peter 3:1-13).

When will it happen? While we can't know the exact time of His coming, we can know when it is near (see Matthew 24:32-36). We'll discuss this more comprehensively later in this chapter.

Where will it happen? He comes from heaven, with the clouds, to this earth (see 1 Thessalonians 4:16, 17; Revelation 1:7).

Why will it happen? Jesus is coming to "gather his elect" (Matthew 24:31).

How will it happen? This same Jesus "will come back in the same way you have seen him go into heaven" (Acts 1:11). That is, the same physical person who ate with the disciples, who allowed them to touch the wounds the nails and spear had left, will return from heaven in the clouds as He ascended.

When Jesus warned about the deceptions linked to His return, He specifically pointed out the need to beware of claims that His second advent would be a secret event:

> So if anyone tells you, "There he is, out in the desert," do not go out; or, "Here he is, in the inner rooms," do not believe it. For as lightning that comes from the east is visible even in the west, so will be the coming of the Son of Man. . . .
>
> At that time the sign of the Son of Man will appear in the sky, and all the nations of the earth will mourn. They will see the Son of Man coming on the clouds of the sky, with power and great glory (Matthew 24:26, 27, 30).

John the Revelator also depicts the universal impact of His coming: "He is coming with the clouds, and every eye will see Him, even those who pierced him; and all the peoples of the earth [who have opposed Him] will mourn because of Him" (Revelation 1:7).

Many other biblical passages testify to the impact of this event. For instance, 1 Thessalonians 4:16 says, "The Lord himself shall descend from heaven with a shout, with the voice of the archangel, and with the trumpet of God" (KJV). And Matthew pictures Jesus coming "in his glory, and all the angels with him" and "in his Father's glory" (Matthew 25:31; 16:27).

When Will Jesus Come?

Expectation of Jesus' return has particularly characterized Seventh-day Adventists. For some 150 years, we've proclaimed the presence of the "last days" and have looked for the realization of Jesus' words: "Behold, I come quickly" (Revelation 22:12, KJV). The questions resonate in our minds: When will Jesus' promise to return meet its fulfillment? Where are we on the time line that runs from the crucifixion to the final resurrection?

Matthew 24 records Jesus' major discussion of His return. In that talk, He warned His disciples that His coming would be unexpected—no one would know the day or hour (see verses 36-44). But He also listed "signs" that would mark the time of His coming. He said that when we see these things, we could "know that it is near, right at the door" (verse 33).

What are some of the signs Jesus listed? He spoke of several in the natural world, particularly a darkening of the sun and moon and a great star shower. The signs in the sun and moon took place on May 19, 1780, when a strange darkness covered most of northeastern North America, blotting out the light of the sun. A full moon rose at 9:00 p.m. but was not seen until midnight. And when it did appear, it was red as blood.

The great meteor shower of November 13, 1833, fulfilled Jesus' prediction of a sign in the stars. This was the most extensive display of falling stars on record. Some people have estimated meteors fell at the rate of sixty thousand per hour.

Revelation 6:12 mentions another sign—a great earthquake which was to precede the signs in the sun, moon, and stars. On November 1, 1755, a tremendous earthquake struck Lisbon, killing some sixty thousand people.

There are two reasons we should take these events seriously as signs marking Jesus' advent. First, they came at the time they were supposed to in the prophetic scheme. And second, their impact on the thought of the time. *All* of these events stirred the consciences of those who witnessed them. And they gave an impetus to the study of prophecy and sparked a religious movement that in itself has been a fulfillment of prophecies related to Jesus' return—a movement that has reached to our day.

Jesus also said, "And this gospel of the kingdom will be preached in the whole world as a testimony to all nations, and then the end will come" (Matthew 24:14). While more a prediction than a sign, it also must be fulfilled before His return.

Through a large part of this century, communism, officially atheistic, dominated many countries of the world and prevented Christian work, to a large extent, from being done in those countries. With the fall of communism, most of these countries are wide open and particularly receptive to the Christian message. Even those few countries still officially communist have softened their opposition to religion.

Obviously, Christians still have work to do in many parts of the world. But this prediction is much nearer fulfillment than it was just a few years ago—and modern means of communication suggest that under the right circumstances, it could be fulfilled in very short order.

The Bridegroom Delayed

So fulfillment of the signs that were to precede Christ's return tells us that it's near. But the Christian church has been looking for His coming for two thousand years. That's a long time. In fact, its been so long that Christians face the danger of losing their sense of its nearness.

Jesus knew this danger. After He listed the signs, He told the story of ten virgins who had been invited to meet and join a wedding party as it passed by. Five of them, He said, were foolish, and five were wise. What separated the wise from the foolish was how prepared they were to wait for a bridegroom who "was delayed" (Matthew 25:5, RSV).

None of the virgins had expected the delay, but five of them were prepared for any eventuality. They had secured sufficient oil to sustain a bright flame in their lamps, while the foolish virgins didn't have enough. When the bridegroom came, the wise virgins, with lamps aglow, entered into the wedding banquet, while the foolish, having gone to get more oil, missed the feast. Jesus ends the parable with the warning, "Watch therefore, for you know neither the day nor the hour" (Matthew 25:13, RSV).

We can easily be diverted from the message of the second coming. Perhaps the most dangerous diversion is that of becoming caught up in the affairs of daily living. Jesus told the story of a farmer who rented a field. As he was working that field, he found a buried treasure. The treasure was immensely valuable, but as long as the field belonged to someone else, it wasn't legally his. So, Jesus said, the farmer sold everything he possessed and bought the field. He didn't mind doing that because it enabled him to obtain the treasure (see Matthew 13:44).

Similarly, knowing Jesus, "obtaining" Him, being ready to meet Him when He returns, is worth the sacrifice of all we have. Nothing we have is worth keeping if it distracts us from Jesus' coming.

But it's not only immersion in the affairs of life that can distract us from the preparation of heart necessary to be ready to meet Him. An unwarranted focus on the time of His return can do the same. As we get closer and closer to the year 2000, we can expect many would-be prophets and prognosticators to manipulate scriptural dates, times, and seasons to come up with dates for the Lord's return. While Jesus Himself gave us signs of its nearness and told us to watch, He also said that no one knows the day nor the hour of His coming: "But of that day or that hour no one knows, not even the angels in heaven, nor the Son, but only the Father" (Mark 13:32).

I am sure that the goal of most of these date publishers is to awaken people to the imminence of the Lord's return, but let us not be beguiled by fascination with the sensational and miss our focus on the Person who is returning. There are those who are more interested in establishing the *time* of His return than teaching the *hope* of His return. When our focus is on signs rather than the Sign Giver, we have missed the message of the advent.

When a scheduled airline flight wings its way toward its destination, the flight controller knows all the details of the trip. He or she knows exactly where it was, is, and will be at various stages of the flight, including when it departed and when it will arrive. A young woman whose fiancé is on the aircraft may know little about the flight other than its approximate time of arrival. But that's enough for her. She is overjoyed at the prospect of meeting one particular passenger on the plane! While the flight controller has much more information about the flight than the young woman has, the controller isn't very excited about the flight because he or she doesn't know anyone on the plane. Knowing all the details of Christ's coming doesn't compare with having a heart full of expectation because of the Person who is coming.

What is it like to wait for Jesus? Being separated from Him is like being away from home for an extended period. When we've been traveling, why are we eager to return home? Is it primarily because we miss our house, its furnishings, its comforts, or its setting? No! The desire to be home is the desire to be with those we love—our spouse, our children, or other members of our family.

Similarly, how we wait for people depends on whom we wait for. Think of how you might wait for the bill collector as compared to how you waited for the first glimpse of your beloved on your wedding day. Or compare your waiting for a long-absent son or daughter with your nervous expectation of a thief who has been breaking into homes in your neighborhood.

The disciples had associated closely with Jesus for three years. Because they knew Him, they loved Him—and consequently, they were so anxious to be with Him again that they greeted each other with "Maranatha," which means "Come, Lord!" They couldn't wait to see Him again.

The human race has been physically separated from Christ nearly two thousand years now. But just as our anticipation at seeing loved ones increases in proportion to how long we've been separated from them, so the length of our separation from Christ should only make us that much more anxious to see Him. But has it? Does our eagerness to see Him give evidence of how intimately we know Him?

I can think of only one reason some of us don't rejoice in the good news of the second advent. We don't know Jesus yet and haven't accepted His assurance of salvation and promise of eternal life.

The second coming will merely be an abstract doctrine to us as long as the Person who is coming is a remote and abstract biblical character. The second coming will be no more than a cold, dead doctrine, detached from our daily living, as long as the Person who is coming is not living in our hearts. We will not love nor look for the second coming as long as we do not love Jesus or spend time with Him now.

When Jesus ascended to heaven, the hope of being with Him again so motivated the disciples that in a few years they spread the gospel across the Roman Empire. When we know Jesus and desire to see Him again, we will do our best to prepare the way for Him. When we have repented and have assurance in Christ, our witness of Him will convey a conviction of urgency. We won't be able to stand the separation any longer. We will be like those people in Jesus' wedding parable who were "waiting for their master to return from a wedding banquet, so that when he comes and knocks they can immediately open the door for him" (Luke 12:36). Our assurance of our relationship with our Master will lead us to an active, expectant waiting for His return. We will share the good news of His return with others.

God is anxious to join His children, but He doesn't want any to perish. So we have a part to play in the divine conclusion to earth's history: "And this gospel of the kingdom will be preached in the whole world as a testimony to all nations, and then the end will come" (Matthew 24:14).

A Parable

A father once left his four sons and traveled to a distant land to earn his fortune. He was gone a very long time.

At first his sons missed him a lot. But as the months passed, they got used to living without him. He did write them regularly, and for a while after he left, they read his letters. But in time some of them gave up on that.

Years after this father left, he sent a letter to his sons saying that he had indeed made a fortune and that he now wanted to share it with his family. The letter said he was returning and gave a time, airline, and flight number.

Calling the airline office, the sons checked the flight schedules. Sure enough, there was a flight scheduled at that time. It seemed that perhaps, after all this time, he might actually be coming home.

Eventually, the day of the father's return arrived. The eldest son doubted that his father had really made a fortune. He suspected that his dad was returning to live off his sons, so he blocked his father's return completely out of his mind.

The second son, who was busy planning a birthday party for his girlfriend, thought the oldest should be the one to go pick up their dad. So he didn't go either.

The third son had read about the delays that airlines had been experiencing and guessed whoever went to pick the father up might find himself waiting in the airport a long time. He concluded that his dad could find his own way home.

The father had left home when the fourth son was very small, so that son couldn't remember his dad at all. And he hadn't read the letters that his dad had sent. Consequently, he figured he wouldn't recognize his dad even if he did go to the airport. And besides, he thought, since he was the youngest son, it wasn't his responsibility to do such chores.

Well, the father did arrive at the airport. And when he found no one to meet him, he took a taxi home. His arrival caught all four sons by surprise. But when he told them his fortune was to be shared only with those who believed his letter enough to meet him at the airport, there was more than surprise. There was weeping and gnashing of teeth.

Peter warned, "In the last days scoffers will come, scoffing and following their own evil desires. They will say, 'Where is this "coming" he promised?' " (2 Peter 3:3, 4). Others, like the foolish virgins Jesus warned about, will say, "There'll be enough time later to get ready." We must not be among either of these groups. We must realize that *now* is the time to get to know Jesus. *Now* is the time to experience His forgiveness, His grace. *Now* is the time to begin living for Him. As Paul reminded Titus, "The grace of God that brings salvation has appeared to all men. It teaches us to say 'No' to ungodliness and worldly passions, and to live self-controlled, upright, and godly lives in this present age, while we wait for the blessed hope—

the glorious appearing of our great God and Savior, Jesus Christ" (Titus 2:11-13).

Jesus is coming back. Only two classes of people will meet Him at His return: the wise and the foolish. The latter will call in terror for the rocks and mountains to fall on them (see Revelation 6:16). Joyfully, the others will say, "Lo, this is our God; we have waited for him, and he will save us" (Isaiah 25:9, KJV). "So do not throw away your confidence; it will be richly rewarded. You need to persevere so that when you have done the will of God, you will receive what he has promised. For in just a very little while, 'he who is coming will come and will not delay' " (Hebrews 10:35-37).

Maranatha! Come, Lord! And may that day hasten!

Yes, we are called to a sense of expectancy in Christ. In the next chapter, we will contemplate the fruits of the victory Christ has won for us—what it means to us now and for the future.

7

Called to Triumph—
in Christ

His victory is our victory.

For weeks beforehand you could feel the excitement in the air. When the day came, you could see the dust before you could see what was stirring it up. You could hear the rumble before you could see the chariots. And all of Rome would turn out, lining the Appian Way—one of the great roads that gave meaning to the saying, "All roads lead to Rome." It was the victory parade of a conquering Roman general. Large floats three to four stories high were pulled or carried along in the parade. They depicted battle victories, fortifications being taken by war machines, enemy temples being set afire, and conquered armies. Some of the floats, covered with gold and ivory, depicted the spoils of war. One commentary describes the scene this way:

> A victorious general was welcomed by government officials at the gates of the imperial city, where the triumphal march began. First came the senators, preceded by a body of magistrates. After the senators came trumpeters, heralding the approach of the victor. Then followed a long train

of carts laden with the spoils of war. Articles of great value, rarity, or beauty were fully exposed to view. There were also white bulls and oxen destined for sacrifice. Here and there incense bearers waved their censers to and fro, perfuming the air. Lions, tigers, elephants, and other strange animals from the captive lands often appeared in the procession. After these came the captive kings, princes, or generals, and a long train of inferior captives, bound and fettered. Next came the great conqueror himself, standing in a splendid chariot. A crown of laurel or gold was upon his head. In one hand he held a branch of laurel, the emblem of victory, and in the other his truncheon or staff of authority" *(Seventh-day Adventist Bible Commentary,* vol. 6, p. 840).

The ancient Romans were not the only ones who held triumphal processions. Jesus did also, riding a donkey into Jerusalem as a conquering king the week of His crucifixion. The multitude that welcomed Jesus into Jerusalem that Sunday of the Passion Week ecstatically extended to Him the welcome of conquering royalty. His triumphal march fulfilled the prophecy of Zechariah: "Rejoice greatly, O daughter of Zion; shout, O daughter of Jerusalem: behold, thy King cometh unto thee: he is just, and having salvation; lowly, and riding upon an ass, and upon a colt the foal of an ass" (Zechariah 9:9, KJV).

But what contrasting processions! The Roman victor would have in tow conquered princes in chains of slavery. Jesus was followed by people whom He had delivered from the slavery of disease and sin, and leading the colt He rode was Lazarus, recently delivered from death itself. Jesus was surrounded, not by beaten captives, but by freed slaves—not by humiliated enemies, but by victorious friends.

The Victories Christ Won

What victories did Christ win that entitled Him to this triumphal procession?

He defeated the "great dragon," "that ancient serpent called the devil, or Satan, who leads the whole world astray" (Revelation 12:9; cf. Matthew 4:11; John 12:31; Colossians 2:15).

And by His resurrection, He defeated death. "Since the children have flesh and blood, he too shared in their humanity so that by his death he might destroy him who holds the power of death—that is, the devil—and free those who all their lives were held in slavery by their fear of death" (Hebrews 2:14, 15).

But Christ's triumph was not something He won to benefit Himself. It was not the kind of prideful victory that we experience on earth. His mission of triumph and victory was for our sakes. His victory—a multifaceted victory—is our victory.

His triumph gives us victory over sin: "What shall we say, then? Shall we go on sinning so that grace may increase? By no means! We died to sin; how can we live in it any longer?" (Romans 6:1, 2).

His triumph gives us victory over the world: "For everyone born of God overcomes the world. This is the victory that has overcome the world, even our faith" (1 John 5:4).

His triumph gives us victory over pain and trouble: "Who shall separate us from the love of Christ? Shall trouble or hardship or persecution or famine or nakedness or danger or sword? As it is written: 'For your sake we face death all day long; we are considered as sheep to be slaughtered.' No, in all these things we are more than conquerors through him who loved us" (Romans 8:35-37).

His triumph gives us victory over death: "When the perishable has been clothed with the imperishable, and the mortal with immortality, then the saying that is written will come true: 'Death has been swallowed up in victory.' 'Where, O death, is your victory? Where, O death, is your sting?' The sting of death is sin, and the power of sin is the law. But thanks be to God! He gives us the victory through our Lord Jesus Christ" (1 Corinthians 15:54-56).

Ellen White writes that because of Jesus' triumph, He "knew that the life of His trusting disciples would be like His, a series of uninterrupted victories, not seen to be such here, but recognized as such in the great hereafter" (*The Desire of Ages*, p. 679). Christians may not appear to triumph. In fact, it may seem that they are being defeated. But the decisive battle has been won, and the victory is ours. As Jesus said, "I will build my church, and the gates of Hades will not overcome it" (Matthew 16:18). As part of the body of Christ, we triumph in Him.

Yet many Christians live lives of fear, doubting their security in Christ, thinking any talk of triumph premature. Unsure of their salvation, they don't know the benefits of the victory Christ has won. They think more about the time of trouble than about the time of grace. They focus more on present pain than on the promised peace.

Satan loves this defeatism. He tries to discourage us by giving us the impression that ours is a lost cause and that victory will forever be out of our reach. He pushes the idea that we can't be overcomers, that it's too hard to measure up. He suggests that only a small minority, the best of the best, will have any chance of salvation.

But Paul used the image of the Roman triumphal procession to encourage the Christians in Corinth—though they certainly still had their problems with sin. He wrote:

> But thanks be to God, who always leads us in triumphal procession in Christ and through us spreads everywhere the fragrance of the knowledge of him. For we are to God the aroma of Christ among those who are being saved and those who are perishing (2 Corinthians 2:14, 15).

And John the Revelator doesn't give the impression that being part of Christ's victory procession need be a distant hope for most people. He says:

> After this I looked and there before me was a great multitude that no one could count, from every nation, tribe, people and language, standing before the throne and in front of the Lamb. They were wearing white robes and were holding palm branches in their hands. And they cried out in a loud voice: "Salvation belongs to our God, who sits on the throne, and to the Lamb" (Revelation 7:9, 10).

John doesn't call the saved a small minority. He doesn't suggest that Christ's victory was effective for only a few. Rather, he proclaims that there "was a great multitude that no one could count." Praise the Lord God who has opened the gates of heaven for everyone who chooses to follow Jesus.

All who find their assurance of salvation in Christ will one day stand with that crowd described in Revelation: "Then I heard what sounded like a great multitude, like the roar of rushing waters and like loud peals of thunder, shouting: 'Hallelujah! For our Lord God Almighty reigns. Let us rejoice and be glad and give him glory! For the wedding of the Lamb has come, and his bride has made herself ready' " (Revelation 19:6, 7).

Part of Christ's Triumphal Procession

How can we be victorious members of Christ's triumphal procession? Let me answer by telling you about another victory procession the Bible describes. That procession is part of a story, and the story makes an important point.

That procession took place during the time Elisha served as prophet in Israel. The Arameans were at war with the Israelites. The Bible says the king of Aram would gather his military officers and plan an ambush against the Israelite forces. But every time he did so, Elisha would warn the king of Israel to avoid the place where the ambush had been set.

The failure of his plans, of course, greatly frustrated the king of Aram. At first, he thought someone among his officers had turned traitor and was passing information to his enemies. When someone told him Elisha was responsible, he sent his army at night to surround Dothan, the city where Elisha was living.

The next morning, Elisha's servant discovered the siege. The prospect of falling into the hands of the enemy terrified him. But Elisha reassured him and then prayed that God would open his eyes. When Elisha's servant looked over the city wall again, he saw that the hills around the city overflowed with horses and chariots of fire. As Elisha put it, " 'Those who are with us are more than those who are with them' " (2 Kings 5:26).

His servant reassured, Elisha prayed that the Aramean forces be struck with blindness, and they were. Then he led these blinded soldiers into Samaria, Israel's capital. How's that for a triumphal procession? Led by Elisha, the prophet, the whole army meekly followed him—no doubt, still wearing their armor. These soldiers, the military might of Israel's enemy, were completely at Israel's mercy.

Well, the story ends with the Israelites putting on a great feast for the Aramean soldiers—whose sight had been restored by that time—and sending them home. Israel's strategy was effective—at least for a while. The Bible says, "So the bands from Aram stopped raiding Israel's territory" (2 Kings 6:23).

The point here, however, is not the triumphal procession. It's what led to that procession. Like Elisha's servant, we sometimes need the reassurance that the battle is the Lord's, that "those who are with us are more than those who are with them."

We've been studying triumphant living in Christ. When we're tempted to feel like failures or to ask, "How can we be triumphant today, given all the problems?" we need to remember that the victory is the Lord's, not ours. God through Jesus Christ won the victory on the cross. When a team wins a victory and earns a trophy, the entire team wins. When we're on Christ's team, His victory is ours as well. So, in the Christian life, it is important that we are on the right team—God's team.

Throughout the Bible we find references to this victory, this triumph. And the message consistently comes through that the victories are not ours, but God's. That is the message of these verses:

■ "For the Lord your God is the one who goes with you to fight for you against your enemies to give you victory" (Deuteronomy 20:4).

■ "The Lord gave David victory wherever he went" (2 Samuel 8:6).

■ "I do not trust in my bow, my sword does not bring me victory; but you give us victory over our enemies, you put our adversaries to shame" (Psalm 44:6, 7).

■ "The horse is made ready for the day of battle, but victory rests with the Lord" (Proverbs 21:31).

The Bible assures us that "though [our] sins be as scarlet, they shall be as white as snow" (Isaiah 1:18, KJV). Praise God, there is power in the blood of Jesus! And not only are we forgiven, but victory is assured, for "he who began a good work in you will carry it on to completion until the day of Christ Jesus" (Philippians 1:6).

When we live a life of repentance and have confident assurance of our relationship with Jesus, we *can* live victorious lives. We're *already* part of His victory parade. And because of Jesus' triumph at the cross, not even death can spoil our victory. Jesus turned that symbol of defeat—the cross—into a symbol of eternal victory.

Christians do have their down times. But when discouragement presses in from all sides, when defeat seems imminent, we must remember that it's not up to us to win the battle. Victory is in the hands of the Lord.

When Jesus Returns

The victory we experience now, in this world, is wonderful. But this victory will be dramatically magnified when Jesus returns in triumph. Imagine the procession of the triumphant, fleeing forever the pain and suffering sin causes!

I love Ellen White's inspired description of Jesus' ascension following His resurrection. I think it suggests what the return to heaven will be like after His second coming:

> As they ascended to the Holy City, the angels who escorted Jesus cried out, "Lift up your heads, O ye gates; and be ye lifted up, ye everlasting doors; and the King of glory shall come in." The angels in the city cried out with rapture, "Who is this King of glory?" The escorting angels answered in triumph, "The Lord strong and mighty, the Lord mighty in battle! Lift up your heads, O ye gates; even lift them up, ye everlasting doors; and the King of glory shall come in!"
>
> Again the waiting angels asked, "Who is this King of glory?" and the escorting angels answered in melodious strains, "The Lord of hosts, he is the King of glory." And the heavenly train passed into the city of God. Then all the heavenly host surrounded their majestic Commander, and with the deepest adoration bowed before Him and cast their glittering crowns at His feet. And then they touched

their golden harps, and in sweet, melodious strains filled all heaven with rich music and songs to the Lamb who was slain, yet lives again in majesty and glory. (*Early Writings*, pp. 190, 191.)

Like the Romans' triumphal processions, Christ's will have its "spoils of victory"—the treasures the conquering army has taken, or recovered, from the enemy. But these spoils are to be destroyed, not put on display or kept. Revelation 21:4 describes them: "He [God] will wipe every tear from their eyes. There will be no more death or mourning or crying or pain, for the old order of things has passed away." The painful and evil aspects of life are among these spoils taken from the enemy to be discarded for eternity, Isaiah says they will not be remembered or come into mind (see chapter 65:16, 17). God Himself promises "trouble will not come a second time" (Nahum 1:9).

But God also offers spoils of His own to those who have chosen the victor's side. And these spoils are worth whatever struggles precede them. Peter indicates that just as the earth was once cleansed by water, it will soon be cleansed by fire—after which God will make it over again (see 2 Peter 3). In that new world, the victorious will build lives for themselves without the fear that others will take the fruits of their efforts (see Isaiah 65:21). God provides a "river of water of life" and a "tree of life" for their sustenance (Revelation 22:1, 2). And the description of the capital city of that new earth makes it obvious that God values His people. He provides for them nothing but the best: the city's walls are made of jasper, its foundations layers of twelve different gemstones, its gates pearl, and the basic structural material used in the rest of the city gold of the purest kind (see Revelation 21 and 22).

But more valuable than the physical riches the future holds are the spiritual and relational. In that new world, we'll be able to enjoy family and friends for eternity. And God will make its capital—the New Jerusalem—the capital city of the universe. That means He'll be here, on the new earth, for eternity—and we, in turn, always will live in His immediate presence. As John the Revelator put it, "Now the dwelling of God is with men, and he will live with them. They will be his people, and God himself will be with them and be their God" (Revelation 21:3).

To understand God, the Creator, we look to the world He has made. But sin has marred this world, so it offers us only a distorted picture. The world He's planned for our future, untouched by sin, tells us more accurately what He's like. It says unequivocally that He is love.

God intends these "spoils" to strengthen us when we are tempted. Hebrews 11:26 says that looking ahead to the reward was what kept Moses faithful to Christ (see also 2 Corinthians 4:16, 17.) This focus on the future even worked for Jesus, "who *for the joy set before him* endured the cross, scorning its shame" (Hebrews 12:2, emphasis supplied).

Going Home

One evening, two citizens lay dying in their homes in a small town. One, a wealthy man, had been a prominent leader of the community. As he lay in his lovely home with the best doctors surrounding him, he whispered despairingly, "I'm leaving home. I'm leaving home."

Across town a solitary figure lay in surroundings bare. Her modest home hardly contained life's essentials. But in her eye was a gleam of faith. Before she died, she whispered triumphantly, "I'm going home. I'm going home." Poor though she was, and unrecognized by the world, she was marching in God's procession of triumph.

There have been similar witnesses to Christ's triumph, similar victories, through the ages. The world would not be any more likely to recognize them than it was hers. It would not inscribe such victories on their tombstones. But they are inscribed where it counts, in our Saviour's book of life. While most of humanity would not judge them triumphant people, they are victorious by God's standards. God's triumphant are the apostolic martyrs Peter and Paul, the martyrs of Nero's persecution, the martyrs of Domitian, the martyrs of the Colosseum, the martyrs of the Reformation, and the thousands of other faithful witnesses and missionaries whose blood blends with the soil of every nation of this earth. All have been victorious through living in Christ.

There is another triumphant group. They are not martyrs of the past, but the triumphant of today. They are those who, during an age of Laodicean laziness and smugness, have followed the counsel of Revelation 3 and have bought "gold refined in the fire, . . . and white clothes to wear, . . . and salve to put on" their eyes (Revelation 3:18). Among this group are young people who have refused to fall to the sin of conformity to an evil society, older people who have held high the banner of truth in an age of compromise, and all people who understand that good times, easy times, pose greater dangers than do times of persecution.

> *"I ask them whence their victory came;*
> *They, with united breath,*
> *Ascribe their conquest to the Lamb,*
> *Their triumph to his death."*
> —Isaac Watts

We've looked at . . .

repentance in Christ,
assurance in Christ,
victory in Christ,
compassion in Christ,
witness in Christ,
expectancy in Christ, and
triumph in Christ.

All these may be ours in Christ. May we all through faith live in Christ so that soon we may be with Him—forever and ever. Amen.

8

Called to Revival— in Christ

The church's great need.

The article that follows represents one of the most powerful appeals made by Ellen G. White for revival and reformation. I include it here because it is so in keeping with the theme and spirit of this book—the privileges and opportunities of those who are called in Christ. I pray that you will prayerfully consider its call to your heart, that it may have its intended effect.—Robert S. Folkenberg

A revival of true godliness among us is the greatest and most urgent of all our needs. To seek this should be our first work. There must be earnest effort to obtain the blessing of the Lord, not because God is not willing to bestow His blessing upon us, but because we are unprepared to receive it. Our heavenly Father is more willing to give His Holy Spirit to them that ask Him than are earthly parents to give good gifts to their children.

But it is our work, by confession, humiliation, repentance, and earnest prayer, to fulfill the conditions upon which God has promised to grant us His blessing. A revival need be expected only in answer to prayer. While the people are so destitute of

God's Holy Spirit, they cannot appreciate the preaching of the Word; but when the Spirit's power touches their hearts, then the discourses given will not be without effect. Guided by the teachings of God's Word, with the manifestation of His Spirit, in the exercise of sound discretion, those who attend our meetings will gain a precious experience, and returning home, will be prepared to exert a healthful influence.

The old standard bearers knew what it was to wrestle with God in prayer, and to enjoy the outpouring of His Spirit. But these are passing off from the stage of action; and who are coming up to fill their places? How is it with the rising generation? Are they converted to God? Are we awake to the work that is going on in the heavenly sanctuary, or are we waiting for some compelling power to come upon the church before we shall arouse? Are we hoping to see the whole church revived? That time will never come.

There are persons in the church who are not converted, and who will not unite in earnest, prevailing prayer. We must enter upon the work individually. We must pray more, and talk less. Iniquity abounds, and the people must be taught not to be satisfied with a form of godliness without the spirit and power. If we are intent upon searching our own hearts, putting away our sins, and correcting our evil tendencies, our souls will not be lifted up unto vanity; we shall be distrustful of ourselves, having an abiding sense that our sufficiency is of God.

We have far more to fear from within than from without. The hindrances to strength and success are far greater from the church itself than from the world. Unbelievers have a right to expect that those who profess to be keeping the commandments of God and the faith of Jesus will do more than any other class to promote and honor, by their consistent lives, by their godly example and their active influence, the cause which they represent. But how often have the professed advocates of the truth proved the greatest obstacle to its advancement! The unbelief indulged, the doubts expressed, the darkness cherished, encourage the presence of evil angels, and open the way for the accomplishment of Satan's devices.

Opening the Door to the Adversary

The adversary of souls is not permitted to read the thoughts of men; but he is a keen observer, and he marks the words; he takes account of actions, and skillfully adapts his temptations to meet the cases of those who place themselves in his power. If we would labor to repress sinful thoughts and feelings, giving them no expression in words or actions, Satan would be defeated; for he could not prepare his specious temptations to meet the case.

But how often do professed Christians, by their lack of self-control, open the door to the adversary of souls! Divisions, and even bitter dissensions which would disgrace any worldly community, are common in the churches, because there is so little effort to control wrong feelings, and to repress every word that Satan can take advantage of. As soon as an alienation of feelings arises, the matter is spread before Satan for his inspection, and the opportunity given for him to use his serpentlike wisdom and skill in dividing and destroying the church.

There is great loss in every dissension. Personal friends of both parties take sides with their respective favorites, and thus the breach is widened. A house divided against itself cannot stand. Criminations and recriminations are engendered and multiplied. Satan and his angels are actively at work to secure a harvest from seed thus sown.

Worldlings look on, and jeeringly exclaim, "Behold how these Christians hate one another! If this is religion, we do not want it." And they look upon themselves and their irreligious characters with great satisfaction. Thus they are confirmed in their impenitence, and Satan exults at his success.

The great deceiver has prepared his wiles for every soul that is not braced for trial and guarded by constant prayer and living faith. As ministers, as Christians, we must work to take the stumbling blocks out of the way. We must remove every obstacle. Let us confess and forsake every sin, that the way of the Lord may be prepared, that He may come into our assemblies and impart His rich grace. The world, the flesh, and the devil must be overcome.

We cannot prepare the way by gaining the friendship of the

world, which is enmity with God; but by His help we can break its seductive influence upon ourselves and upon others. We cannot individually or as a body secure ourselves from the constant temptations of a relentless and determined foe; but in the strength of Jesus we can resist them.

From every member of the church a steady light may shine forth before the world, so that they shall not be led to inquire, What do these people more than others? There can be and must be a withdrawal from conformity to the world, a shunning of all appearance of evil, so that no occasion shall be given for gainsayers. We cannot escape reproach; it will come; but we should be very careful that we are not reproached for our own sins or follies, but for Christ's sake.

There is nothing that Satan fears so much as that the people of God shall clear the way by removing every hindrance, so that the Lord can pour out His Spirit upon a languishing church and an impenitent congregation. If Satan had his way, there would never be another awakening, great or small, to the end of time. But we are not ignorant of his devices. It is possible to resist his power. When the way is prepared for the Spirit of God, the blessing will come. Satan can no more hinder a shower of blessing from descending upon God's people than he can close the windows of heaven that rain cannot come upon the earth. Wicked men and devils cannot hinder the work of God, or shut out His presence from the assemblies of His people, if they will, with subdued, contrite hearts, confess and put away their sins, and in faith claim His promises. Every temptation, every opposing influence, whether open or secret, may be successfully resisted, "not by might, nor by power, but by my spirit, saith the Lord of hosts" (Zech. 4:6).

We Are in the Day of Atonement

We are in the great day of atonement, when our sins are, by confession and repentance, to go beforehand to judgment. God does not now accept a tame, spiritless testimony from His ministers. Such a testimony would not be present truth. The message for this time must be meat in due season to feed the church of God. But Satan has been seeking gradually to rob this message of its power, that the people may not be prepared to stand in the day of the Lord.

In 1844 our great High Priest entered the Most Holy Place of the heavenly sanctuary, to begin the work of the investigative judgment. The cases of the righteous dead have been passing in review before God. When that work shall be completed, judgment is to be pronounced upon the living. How precious, how important are these solemn moments! Each of us has a case pending in the court of heaven. We are individually to be judged according to the deeds done in the body. In the typical service, when the work of atonement was performed by the high priest in the Most Holy Place of the earthly sanctuary, the people were required to afflict their souls before God, and confess their sins, that they might be atoned for and blotted out. Will any less be required of us in this antitypical day of atonement, when Christ in the sanctuary above is pleading in behalf of His people, and the final, irrevocable decision is to be pronounced upon every case?

What is our condition in this fearful and solemn time? Alas, what pride is prevailing in the church, what hypocrisy, what deception, what love of dress, frivolity, and amusement, what desire for the supremacy! All these sins have clouded the mind, so that eternal things have not been discerned. Shall we not search the Scriptures, that we may know where we are in this world's history? Shall we not become intelligent in regard to the work that is being accomplished for us at this time, and the position that we as sinners should occupy while this work of atonement is going forward? If we have any regard for our souls' salvation, we must make a decided change. We must seek the Lord with true penitence; we must with deep contrition of soul confess our sins, that they may be blotted out.

We must no longer remain upon the enchanted ground. We are fast approaching the close of our probation. Let every soul inquire, How do I stand before God? We know not how soon our names may be taken into the lips of Christ, and our cases be finally decided. What, oh, what will these decisions be! Shall we be counted with the righteous, or shall we be numbered with the wicked?

The Church to Arise and Repent

Let the church arise, and repent of her backslidings before God. Let the watchmen awake, and give the trumpet a certain sound. It is a definite warning that we have to proclaim. God commands His servants, "Cry aloud, spare not, lift up thy voice like a trumpet, and shew my people their transgression, and the house of Jacob their sins" (Isa. 58:1). The attention of the people must be gained; unless this can be done, all effort is useless; though an angel from heaven should come down and speak to them, his words would do no more good than if he were speaking into the cold ear of death.

The church must arouse to action. The Spirit of God can never come in until she prepares the way. There should be earnest searching of heart. There should be united, persevering prayer, and through faith a claiming of the promises of God. There should be, not a clothing of the body with sackcloth, as in ancient times, but a deep humiliation of soul. We have not the first reason for self-congratulation and self-exaltation. We should humble ourselves under the mighty hand of God. He will appear to comfort and bless the true seekers.

The work is before us; will we engage in it? We must work fast, we must go steadily forward. We must be preparing for the great day of the Lord. We have no time to lose, no time to be engaged in selfish purposes. The world is to be warned. What are we doing as individuals to bring the light before others? God has left to every man his work; every one has a part to act, and we cannot neglect this work except at the peril of our souls.

O my brethren, will you grieve the Holy Spirit, and cause [Him] to depart? Will you shut out the blessed Saviour, because you are unprepared for His presence? Will you leave souls to perish without the knowledge of the truth, because you love your ease too well to bear the burden that Jesus bore for you? Let us awake out of sleep. "Be sober, be vigilant; because your adversary the devil, as a roaring lion, walketh about, seeking whom he may devour" (1 Peter 5:8).[1]

[A few years later, in another *Review and Herald* article, Mrs.

White returned to the subject of revival and reformation. I close with one paragraph from that piece.]

In many hearts there seems to be scarcely a breath of spiritual life. This makes me very sad. I fear that aggressive warfare against the world, the flesh, and the devil has not been maintained. Shall we cheer on, by a half-dead Christianity, the selfish, covetous spirit of the world, sharing its ungodliness and smiling on its falsehood? Nay! By the grace of God let us be steadfast to the principles of truth, holding firm to the end the beginning of our confidence. We are to be "not slothful in business; fervent in spirit; serving the Lord" (Rom. 12:11). One is our Master, even Christ. To Him we are to look. From Him we are to receive our wisdom. By His grace we are to preserve our integrity, standing before God in meekness and contrition, and representing Him to the world.[2]

---

1. The article was published in the *Review and Herald*, March 22, 1887. It is reprinted in *Selected Messages*, book 1, pp. 121-127.

2. *Selected Messages*, book 1, p. 127 (see also the *Review and Herald*, Feb. 25, 1902).

If you enjoyed this book . . .

and would like to receive additional materials or information, simply indicate your choices, print your name and address, then tear out this page and mail it to:

Pacific Press
P.O. Box 7000
Boise, ID 83707

_____ I would like to purchase a copy of *The Desire of Ages*, the classic book on the life of Christ. (Enclose check or money order for $3.50, payable to Pacific Press.)

_____ I would like a **FREE** set of Bible study guides.

_____ I would like information concerning a free seminar on the book of Revelation in my area.

_____ I would like a list of other books published by Pacific Press.

_____ I would like **FREE** information on other literature related to the topics contained in this book.

(These offers good in the United States and Canada only.)

For further information, call toll free:
Adventist Information Services
1-800-253-3000.